A. Morrison and D. McIntyre
Schools and Socialization

Penguin Books

Penguin Books Ltd, Harmondsworth,
Middlesex, England
Penguin Books Inc, 7110 Ambassador Road,
Baltimore, Md 21207, U.S.A.
Penguin Books Australia Ltd,
Ringwood, Victoria, Australia

First published 1971
Reprinted 1972
Copyright © A. Morrison and D. McIntyre, 1971

Made and printed in Great Britain by
C. Nicholls & Company Ltd, Manchester
Set in Linotype Times

Penguin Science of Behaviour

This book is one of an ambitious project, the Penguin Science of Behaviour, which covers a very wide range of psychological inquiry. Many of the short 'unit' texts are on central teaching topics, while others deal with present theoretical and empirical work which the Editors consider to be important new contributions to psychology. We have kept in mind both the teaching divisions of psychology and also the needs of psychology at work. For readers working with children, for example, some of the units in the field of Developmental Psychology will deal with psychological techniques in testing children, other units will deal with work on cognitive growth. For academic psychologists, there will be units in well-established areas such as Learning and Perception, but also units which do not fall neatly under any one heading, or which are thought of as 'applied', but which nevertheless are highly relevant to psychology as a whole.

The project is published in short units for two main reasons. Firstly, a large range of short texts at inexpensive prices gives the teacher a flexibility in planning his course and recommending texts for it. Secondly, the pace at which important new work is published requires the project to be adaptable. Our plan allows a unit to be revised or a fresh unit to be added, with maximum speed and minimal cost to the reader.

Above all, for students, the different viewpoints of many authors, sometimes overlapping, sometimes in contradiction, and the range of topics Editors have selected will reveal the complexity and diversity which exist beyond the necessarily conventional headings of an introductory course.

B.M.F.

Contents

Editorial Foreword

This volume is in the Social Psychology section of the Science of Behaviour series. In this part of the series a number of volumes are planned which will give a comprehensive coverage of Social Psychology, each written by active research workers, and providing an up-to-date and rigorous account of different parts of the subject. There has been an explosive growth of research in Social Psychology in recent years, and the subject has broken out of its early preoccupation with the laboratory to study social behaviour in a variety of social settings. These volumes will differ somewhat from most existing textbooks: in addition to citing laboratory experiments they will cite field studies, and deal with the details and complexities of the phenomena as they occur in the outside world. Links will be established with other disciplines, such as sociology, anthropology, animal behaviour, linguistics, and other branches of psychology, where relevant. As well as being useful to students, these monographs should therefore be of interest to a wide public.

The authors of this volume brought out a previous book in the same series – *Teachers and Teaching* – that dealt with the social skills of teachers, and social behaviour in the classroom. In *Schools and Socialization* they turn to a different aspect of the social psychology of education – the ways in which the school affects the child. They demonstrate the effect of the school on academic performance, and how this is affected by other factors such as social class, type of school and parental influence. They show how the school affects moral development, social behaviour, political outlook, attitudes to other countries and choice of occupation. The authors report a great deal of very interesting research, and extend the topic of 'socialization' beyond what is normally included in books on Social Psychology.

The book should be of great interest to all involved in education. It shows a lot of unexpected effects of the educational process, and provides evidence on the effects of different kinds of school both on academic performance and in other spheres of behaviour.

M.A.

Preface

Children grow up in several environments. Home, school and community are the settings for social and intellectual experiences from which they acquire and develop the skills, attitudes and attachments which characterize them as individuals and shape their choice and performance of adult roles. This book is about the agencies, practices and processes involved in socialization and, in particular, about the ways in which schools and other educational institutions, through their teachers, curricula and organization, deliberately or incidentally influence the young.

Schools are in a strong position to exert influence upon their students. In part this stems from their specialized functions and expertise concerning scholastic and technical instruction; it comes also from the opportunities created by formal organization to introduce students to forms of authority and to social and working relationships which might otherwise not be experienced; from educational policies which lead to achievement differentiation and selection, affecting preparation for social and occupational roles; and from the bringing together of individuals into informal social systems. Some of this influence is specific and overt, operating through deliberate instruction to more or less determined objectives; some is more diffuse and less systematic, but may have pervasive effects.

Our emphasis then is upon schools and their students, and upon findings from research in social psychology and education about educational influence. However, it makes little sense to discuss schools in isolation from the other agencies of socialization. They are neither the first nor necessarily among the more important agencies. Nor is their degree of influence the same for every individual for all aspects of behaviour and attitudes, since child rearing and community experiences interact in complicated ways with response to school. Consequently, we have approached each of our topics through a broad discussion of practices and processes before turning to the evidence on schools. By doing this we hope that educational influence has been put in its proper perspective and that its limitations can be appreciated.

The book deals with four major areas of socialization, chosen to represent areas of skills and attitudes which are to varying degrees the concern of schools, open to educational influence and affected by different school factors. The first chapter, on academic performance, comes closest to the obvious objectives of schools and to the direct influence of teachers and the curriculum. Chapter 2 on interpersonal behaviour lays more stress upon the informal and peer-group aspects of schools and upon the important but ill-understood influences upon short-term and more persisting social behaviour. Chapter 3 on politics and school discusses an area of attitudes which has often in the past had only a limited educational treatment. This book gives an opportunity to introduce a great deal of fairly recent research by American political scientists which seems relevant both to the curriculum and to the diffuse influences of schools upon students' orientations to the political system. The part played by schools in affecting the subsequent careers and occupations of students is then discussed in the last chapter.

Finally, we should like to thank all those who have helped us with our work, particularly those whose research helps to show some of the characteristics of social and educational influence and interaction, and incidentally brings out how little we understand about some aspects of our schools.

A.M. and D.Mc.I.

1 Social Factors Affecting Academic Success

As this book is about ways in which children's social environments influence aspects of their development to which education is particularly relevant, it is appropriate to start by considering factors affecting the achievement of what is generally seen to be the primary goal of formal education, academic success.

The criteria on which we assess 'academic success' must depend on the definition which we choose for this concept. We may take either a sociological or a psychological perspective; both have their limitations. From a sociological viewpoint, the most important determinant of a person's adult status in Western societies such as Britain and the USA is generally his <u>occupation</u>; and entry to an ever-increasing number of occupations is dependent upon academic qualifications such as school-leaving certificates and university degrees. Thus if academic success is judged in terms of the social status to which it is likely to lead, major criteria must be the level, grade and number of such formal qualifications which a person has obtained. Another factor which is often relevant when people are competing for occupational positions is the academic selectivity of the educational institutions one has attended, irrespective of the qualifications one has obtained there: to have attended university is in itself valuable; to have been to Oxford is even better. A third possible type of criterion of academic success on the grounds of its value in gaining relatively high-status jobs is educational longevity, the number of years one has continued one's full-time education beyond the minimum school leaving age.

It is clearly inadequate, however, to define academic

success solely in terms of educational outcomes which affect
occupational status, if only because many non-academic
acquisitions at school, such as social skills, attitudes and
personal contacts, may have considerable bearing on occupational careers. What is distinctive about the criteria of
academic success suggested above is that not only are they
likely in fact to affect the status of occupations entered but
that they are publicly approved bases for discriminating
among people in the allocation of occupations; furthermore, the relevant information is publicly verifiable. Thus,
even where an individual does not enter an occupation appropriate to his level of academic success, he can feel that
he has already earned and become entitled to an equivalent
social status, and in many contexts such status may be
accorded to him.

From a psychological viewpoint, academic success might
be defined in terms of the acquisition of different kinds of
knowledge and cognitive skills. In some respects the multi-
dimensional description which one could then have would
be theoretically most satisfactory. It would, however, make
comparisons among people extremely difficult; and in practice, the evidence usually available is only of attainments in
one or two aspects of schoolwork or of 'average' attainments, with the particular skills assessed not generally being
specified. Such crude measures of attainment are closely
related to the formal academic qualifications discussed
above. But it seems useful to retain a distinction between
the two perspectives on 'academic success', using this term
for the sociological definition, in contrast to the 'cognitive
attainment' which concerns the psychologist. On the one
hand, success involves more than attainment: it involves
the motivation which allows one to capitalize upon one's
education. On the other hand, where the judgements of
others intervene, attainment may not always be rewarded
with success. It would only be in a perfectly efficient merito-
cratic society that cognitive attainment and academic success would be synonymous.

During childhood and adolescence, most of the social

influences upon individuals can be categorized as being associated either with home or with school environments; and this chapter is divided into two major sections dealing respectively with these two sets of potentially influential factors. From the outset, however, it should be clear that the distinction is one more of convenience than of explanatory value. For one thing, the characteristics of the school one attends tend to vary according to one's home background. For another, it is not in themselves but in relation to his experiences at school that many of the distinctive characteristics of a child's home environment may be seen to influence his academic success.

The home environment

In attempting to analyse the influence of the home upon educational attainment and success, we must face some fundamental methodological problems. What sort of explanations are desirable and what sort are possible? At the most general level we find that success is related to social class: the children of people in professional and managerial occupations, for example, are much more likely to be successful than the children of unskilled manual workers. This is interesting information, but obviously we want to go on to ask why this is so. At this point two broadly different approaches are possible.

We may attempt to measure many different aspects of home environment and discover the extent to which each of these is correlated with success criteria. But most of the correlates of success are found to be correlated with social class and with one another: how is the influence of each to be distinguished? Factor X may be correlated with the criterion not because the two are causatively related but because both are correlated with factor Y. The obvious solution to such a problem is to set up carefully designed experiments in which some factors are controlled and others are applied in prescribed ways to different samples of children. In most cases, however, there are overwhelming moral objections to this sort of procedure. And even

where this is not so, experiments are often quite imprac-
ticable: such variables as parents' aspirations for their
children's future are not easily susceptible to a social scientist's control. Using surveys rather than experiments, it is
possible to overcome these problems to some extent by a
careful choice of samples and the use of various statistical
techniques. At best, though, it is only possible to say which
variables are most closely related to success, not which factors lead to differences in success.

An additional limitation of statistical surveys aimed at
isolating the effects of different factors, is that the influence
of any one factor is likely to depend on the total social
context in which it operates. Family size, for example, is
likely to have different implications for poor and rich families. And it is virtually impossible to consider statistically
the effects of all possible interactions of a large number of
variables. Perhaps it is better to consider all the inter-
related correlates of success as more or less reliable symptoms of total patterns of family life which are, or are not,
conducive to success, rather than as factors which each
exert their independent influence. From this point of view,
the more fruitful approach would be to attempt to describe
and categorize such patterns of family life, to discover how
far, and in what way, each affects success, and to identify
the conditions in which each pattern is likely to occur. This
approach, while perhaps more likely to lead us to a description of the processes whereby home environment
affects success, requires much more extensive empirical investigation than the statistical survey approach, and is more
dependent on sociological and psychological theory. It is,
therefore, likely to be slower in providing firmly established
conclusions.

In this chapter we shall consider first the results of social-
class analyses, then those obtained by statistical surveys
aimed at isolating those variables most related to success and,
thirdly, evidence about the effects of different types of family
life. First, however, we must consider a problem which arises
in interpreting much of the relevant evidence: how can we

distinguish between the effects of environmental variations and those of genetic differences? This problem presents itself most commonly in terms of the difficulty of knowing what place to give to differences in measured intelligence.

The place of 'intelligence'

Until recently, most psychologists took the view that differences in intelligence are almost entirely innately determined, environmental factors being of very minor importance. On this assumption, Fraser (1959) attempted to assess the effects of various aspects of the home environment on attainment by finding how much more each aspect was correlated with attainment than with intelligence. That both intelligence and attainment were correlated with parental income, for example, merely showed that income was influenced by parental characteristics which, inherited by their children, affected their attainment. Only the *difference* between the two correlations indicated whether income affected attainment.

Another view is that intelligence is simply one important aspect of attainment, which, although less related to the specific instruction received in school, is also dependent on environmental factors and especially upon education. Taking this view, Douglas (1964) assessed the progress of the pupils in his study by averaging their scores on tests of intelligence and of attainment in school subjects. 'With a few exceptions,' he said, 'the circumstances which are associated with a deterioration in the scores for the achievement tests are equally associated with a deterioration in the mental ability scores, and so there seemed no point in making a distinction between the two types of test used in this study' (Douglas, 1964, p.8).

While Fraser and Douglas may represent extreme positions, the fact that their studies have been among the most influential undertaken in Britain indicates the widely divergent attitudes to intelligence. Since such different approaches inevitably lead to different conclusions, one is forced to consider the relative merits of the two positions.

Unfortunately the heredity–environment controversy about intelligence is still hotly debated even among the highest authorities on the subject (e.g. Hunt, 1969; Jensen, 1969); but it does seem almost certain that both hereditary and environmental factors are involved. On one side, there is evidence such as the findings that between monozygotic twins – virtually identical genetically – reared apart, IQs are typically correlated about 0·75, whereas the correlation between the IQs of dyzygotic twins reared together tends to be about 0·53. Although interpretation of such results is not so straightforward as it at first appears, 'the general opinion of most authorities, however, seems to be that a substantial degree of genetic determination of measured intelligence can hardly be denied' (Butcher, 1968, p.157). On the other side, there is ample evidence that environmental factors also influence intelligence. In some cases there are considerable differences between the IQs of monozygotic twins raised apart; and the IQs of unrelated people reared together are commonly found to be significantly, if not highly, correlated. We are, therefore, left with the question of the relative importance of environmental and genetic factors.

There cannot, however, be any simple answer to this question. In any society, environmental and hereditary factors are bound to interact in many different ways. For example, parents of above average intelligence are likely both to have children who innately tend to be above average in intelligence and also to provide these children with an environment conducive to the development of above average intelligence. Furthermore, according as environmental variations are greater or less at different times and in different societies, so in general will the environmental component account for a respectively increased or decreased proportion of the variation in intelligence among the population.

An alternative to the traditional psychometric approach to intelligence is Piaget's emphasis on the way in which an individual's intelligence develops. Building on Piaget's work, Hunt (1961) has fruitfully reformulated the heredity–environment controversy by asking what conditions and experiences are necessary or valuable for the development of intelligence. There is a marked lack of evidence with which to answer this fundamental question. What is quite certain, however, is that there *are* conditions in which intelligence does not develop 'normally'. Studies of people in isolated and culturally impoverished communities in Britain and the United States have shown that while younger children have IQs not much below the national norm, average IQ decreases markedly and systematically with age. Such environments, it would appear, do not provide the stimuli necessary for the development of the intelligence acquired by most people in the mainstream of modern society.

Abstracting from a very large number of cross-sectional comparisons of groups or individuals, one may provisionally identify those aspects of the social environment which appear to have most effect upon intelligence. Any such list of influential features of the environment turns out to be much the same whether one is considering intelligence or school attainment, though the relative importance of various environmental conditions is not the same for different aspects of ability or attainment (Vernon, 1969; Wiseman, 1964). The effects of one environmental variable may be most apparent on reading test scores, those of another on arithmetic test scores and those of a third on scores in a verbal intelligence test. This being so, there seems little justification for concluding, as Fraser does, that those features of the home environment which most influence school progress can be identified by taking correlations of environmental variables with intelligence as a 'base-line' against which correlations with attainment measures should be compared. Hereditary factors must almost certainly be assumed to be a major source of individual differences in attainment, but to compare attainment with intelligence is not an adequate way of taking account of this and is likely to lead to distorted conclusions.

If this is so, we are left with the problem of distinguishing genetic from environmental influences upon attainment. It is a problem which cannot at present be solved, except to some extent when one has unusual samples such as identical twins or children separated from their mothers at birth. With regard to much of the evidence to be presented in this chapter it is, therefore, necessary to ask 'But could this be the result of genetic differences?' One should presumably be least inclined to suspect the influence of such differences when a convincing explanation can be offered of the social processes underlying apparent environmental influences upon success. It seems to us that a scientific and educationally fruitful attitude is to hypothesize that apparent environmental influences are in fact what they seem; deliberate and informed attempts can then be made to alter characteristics of the environment inimical to success, and only when all such attempts fail should the hypotheses be rejected.

Social class

Because social inequalities in income, power and prestige are all closely related to occupation, social class is most commonly described in terms of occupational categories. Various systems of categorization are used, however, so that the different results mentioned in this section are not always comparable with one another. The situation is further complicated by the use in some cases of other variables such as the number of years of formal education a person has received. This lack of comparability does not, however, obscure the general pattern of how social class is related to success at various levels of education.

Attainment is closely related to social class from the early years of primary school. Among a virtually representative sample of several thousand English seven year olds (Kellmer Pringle, Butler and Davis, 1966), 55 per cent of those from social classes I and II (Registrar-General's Scale) were found to be 'good readers' as opposed to only 34 per cent of those from classes III, IV and V. Similar differences were apparent for arithmetic ability, though not so great. Even before this age, however, many children have experienced success or failure. Jackson (1964) found that, of a sample of 660 schools in England and Wales large enough for streaming to be possible, 74 per cent had already streamed pupils by the age of seven. Although the social-class composition of the streams which he reports is for eleven year olds, the consistent finding that changes of stream are very rare (Douglas, 1964, found an annual rate of 2·3 per cent) means that the initial composition must have been very similar. Social class and school stream were closely related; for example 55 per cent of the children of professional and managerial workers in four-stream schools were in A stream and 18 per cent in C or D stream, as opposed to 14 per cent and 62 per cent respectively for the children of unskilled manual workers.

Social-class differences in attainment increase as children grow older. Douglas (1964), in his longitudinal study of a random sample of all children born in Britain in one week in 1946, found that differences between the mean attainments of the children of manual and non-manual workers increased between the ages of eight and eleven. Irrespective of the level of attainment, significant differences appeared at age eleven between children of the two classes who had been equal in attainment at age eight.

Up to the present, a major criterion of educational success in Britain has been the type of secondary school to which one gains entry. Like several other investigators, Douglas found that children of non-manual workers were several times more likely than those of manual workers to gain a grammar-school place. Moreover he found that these class differences could not entirely be explained by differences in scores on his ability and attainment tests at age eleven. Especially in those areas where a relatively small number of grammar-school places were available, upper-middle-class children[1] obtained, relative to others, many

1. Douglas subdivided the non-manual or middle class and the manual or working class into upper and lower according to the childhood background and education of both parents.

more places than their test scores warranted; these differences are shown in Table 1. Other factors in the selection procedures, such as parental enthusiasm for grammar-school education and teachers' assessments of likely success in grammar schools, clearly weighed heavily against the children of manual workers.

Table 1
Children in Each Social Class Entering Grammar Schools as a Percentage of Those 'Expected' to Do so on the Basis of Their Test Scores and of Upper-Middle-Class Results (from Douglas, 1964, p. 153)

Social class	Children in LEAs where over one-fifth go to grammar schools	Children in LEAs where one-fifth or under go to grammar schools
Non-manual		
Upper	100	100
Lower	99	72
Manual		
Upper	85	60
Lower	72	52

In secondary schools it is more difficult to compare attainment because of the different types of school and the variety of courses within each type of school. Attempts to assess the attainment of a complete age-group, therefore, tend to be limited to the 'basic' subjects of English and arithmetic/mathematics. In the continuation of Douglas's longitudinal study into the secondary-school stage (Douglas, Ross and Simpson, 1968), it was found that among pupils in both selective and secondary-modern schools there was a continued tendency for the children of non-manual workers to pull ahead between the ages of eleven and fifteen both in reading and mathematics. Because of middle-class success in gaining entry to selective schools, the even more marked tendency for the test scores of pupils at selective schools to improve relative to those of others adds to the increasing difference in mean attainment between the classes.

The major criterion of success in secondary school is the number and level of passes in external exams. Until recently, however, the only relevant exams in England have been those for the General Certificate of Education, attempted by only a minority of pupils. The report by the Central Advisory Council for Education (England) on *Early Leaving* (1954) showed that success in GCE exams was as closely related to a pupil's social class as to his assessed ability at eleven. For example, 67 per cent of those from social class I among the least able third of entrants obtained at least three O-level passes, a standard achieved by only 46 per cent of those from social class V among the most able third. Table 2 shows that much the same was true in 1962, even when pupils were classified on ability at fifteen. And, as the *Robbins Report* (1963, app. 1, pt 2) showed, the children of manual workers are at an even greater disadvantage in obtaining A-level passes.

Social class is also closely related to school leaving age. As the data of Table 2 shows, working-class children are more likely to leave school before taking O-level exams; those who do stay at school are less likely to be successful; and, among those who are successful, working-class children are less likely to stay on at school for a sixth-year course.

By the age of eighteen, class differences in school leaving age appear to have cancelled out the effects of other class influences upon attainment. Among pupils leaving school aged eighteen or more, no systematic differences are apparent in the proportion of pupils from each social class who obtain two or more A-level passes (*Robbins Report*, 1963, app.1). Similarly, available evidence indicates that, in Britain as a whole, there are no differences in the success rate of students from different social classes at universities. None the less, social class does affect chances of *entry* to university. Whether this is because of class differences in the proportion of qualified school-leavers who apply for university courses, or because a greater proportion of working-class applicants are rejected, does not appear to have been investigated.

Table 2
Percentage Proportions Staying at School and Gaining Certificates, Related to Ability and Social Class (from Douglas, Ross and Simpson, 1968, p. 204)

| Social class | Average test score at 15 years | | | | |
	60 and over	55–9	50–54	45–49	44 and less
Per cent completing session 1961–2 (year for O-level exams)					
Middle					
Upper	97	93	86	69	40
Lower	94	79	59	36	17
Manual					
Upper	90	67	35	22	6
Lower	80	46	27	12	3
Per cent starting session 1962–3					
Middle					
Upper	90	82	71	42	20
Lower	78	52	37	20	8
Manual					
Upper	67	43	20	10	3
Lower	50	20	12	4	2
Per cent gaining certificates					
Middle					
Upper	94	79	54	27	20
Lower	87	59	38	13	1
Manual					
Upper	86	45	17	5	0
Lower	69	31	12	2	0

In summary, social class is related to educational success in four distinct ways: ability at age of entry to school; attainment in school subjects, when initial ability differences are held constant; age of leaving, irrespective of attainment; and, certainly in secondary-school selection and probably at other stages, in judgements made by teachers and others, irrespective of attainment.

Correlates of success in the home environment

Social class may be considered as a 'summarizing' variable. The different occupations of fathers are not likely in themselves to account for the marked differences in success which we have observed. These differences result rather from the many variations in material conditions, in attitudes and values, and generally in the ways in which families live, that are associated with socio-economic status. Which of these inter-related variations in home environment, it may be asked, have most influence upon success?

The basic correlational approach to this question was well exemplified by Fraser's (1959) investigation in Aberdeen. A measure of the secondary-school attainment of 427 pupils from six schools, representative of their age-group in both intelligence and social class, was calculated from their marks in school examinations. This was correlated with ratings of several aspects of their home backgrounds based on visits to the homes and interviews with the parents; correlations with scores on a verbal intelligence test were also calculated. Results were as in Table 3.

Table 3
Correlations of Ratings of Home Environment with Attainment and IQ (from Fraser, 1959)

	Correlation with attainment	Correlation with IQ
Parents' education	0·49	0·42
Parents' general book reading	0·33	0·28
Magazine and newspaper reading	0·40	0·38
Income	0·44	0·35
Family size	0·46	0·40
Living space	0·45	0·36
Parents' attitudes to child's education and future employment	0·39	0·30
Parental encouragement (teachers' rating)	0·66	0·60
General impression of home environment (emotional atmosphere)	0·46	0·39

In addition it was found that children with 'abnormal home backgrounds' – those without two parents living in reasonable harmony – tended to be below average in attainment, but those whose mothers went out to work did not. As mentioned earlier, Fraser interpreted these results by comparing the attainment correlations with the IQ correlations. Thus, for example, the correlation of 0·44 between income and attainment was compared with the correlation of 0·35 between income and IQ. These correlations show a small but definite tendency for both IQ and attainment to be higher on average for families with relatively large incomes than for those with smaller incomes; but the connection between attainment and income is slightly stronger than between IQ and income. The results for family size are very similar – the larger the family, the lower attainment and IQ tend to be – but there is slightly less difference between the two correlations. Fraser argued that since the correlations between IQ and environmental factors should be explained in terms of heredity (e.g. children with low IQs tend to have parents with relatively low IQs who tend, because of this, to have large families and to earn relatively little) and since the attainment correlations can largely be explained on the same grounds, only the difference between the two correlations for each variable should be considered. Therefore, income had more influence on attainment than did family size; and the other most influential factors, she concluded, were parents' attitudes, living space and abnormal background.

It would be as valid and as dangerous, in view of our uncertainty about the effects of heredity on intelligence, to interpret the results in a much simpler way, concluding that the factors which most influenced attainment were those most highly correlated with it. Another equally important factor which makes it impossible to conclude anything from this evidence is the certainty that the environmental variables are not independent. For example, the correlation between income and attainment could be entirely due to the effects of differences in parents' education affecting both their own employment and the educational help they gave their children. Before even tentative conclusions can be reached, account must be taken of the correlations among environmental variables.

One fruitful way of dealing with this problem is by the technique of multiple regression whereby one can discover the independent contribution which each of a number of variables can make to the prediction of a criterion variable. This technique was used in an investigation undertaken for the Plowden Committee on primary education (Peaker, 1967). A stratified random sample of over three thousand children in three age-groups from English primary schools were tested on standardized reading tests and rated on their general attainment by their teachers. Environmental variables, 104 in all, were grouped in three categories – parental attitudes (including, rather oddly, the 'literacy' of the home), home circumstances and school variables. Twelve separate analyses were carried out for boys and girls, the three age-groups and variations between and within schools. For within-schools analyses the criterion was the teacher's rating and for between-schools analyses it was the score on the reading test. In each analysis, the variable most highly correlated with the criterion was first selected, then that one of the remainder which together with the first could best predict criterion scores; in this way, successive variables were selected according to the extent to which they could improve the prediction until no further significant improvements could be made.

The major results with regard to home environment of this very thorough investigation were:

1. In general, variations in parental attitudes could account for much more of the variation in attainment than could either of the other two categories of variables, both for differences between schools and for differences within schools.

2. The three specific variables which accounted for most variation in attainment, all of them in the 'parental

attitudes' category, were: *educational aspirations, literacy of the home* and *parental interest in the child's school-work.*

3. The aspects of home circumstances which accounted for most variation in attainment were: *the physical amenities of the home, the number of dependent children* (negatively correlated with attainment), *father's occupation* and *parents' education.* Par Edul Behavs

4. Parental attitudes were more important for older than for younger pupils and more important for boys than for girls.

5. Home circumstances were more important for girls than for boys.

Peaker also showed that variation in parental attitudes was largely independent of variation in home circumstances.

A second technique of multivariate analysis for identifying crucial environmental variables is factor analysis, a technique used by Wiseman (1964, 1967) in his important Manchester studies. In this, the correlations among all the variables are analysed in terms of a small number of independent dimensions, or factors, chosen so as to show the patterns of intercorrelation as clearly as possible. The extent to which each of the original variables is associated with each of the dimensions is given by its 'factor loading'; and the nature of the variation on each dimension is discovered by examining the variables with high loadings on it to see what they have in common. Compared with regression analysis this approach does not indicate so clearly which *specific* environmental variables contribute most to predicting attainment; what it does is to establish several *general* ways in which environments do vary, and how each of these general dimensions of variation is related to attainment. Conclusions, therefore, tend to be more reliable in that each depends on several measures of the environment rather than just one. Of course the dimensions which emerge depend upon which aspects of the environment have been measured in the first place.

One of the distinctive features of Wiseman's research has been his use of the school and the city ward as units of study, rather than the individual child. The measures of attainment used have similarly been measures for the school or ward, such as average scores on tests and proportions of 'bright' and 'backward' children. A result of this research design is that the results must emphasize environmental variations from one part of a city to another rather than those between homes within each area.

Two investigations were conducted among fourteen-year-old pupils in Manchester secondary-modern schools (Wiseman, 1964). In the first, he found that variations in backwardness were almost entirely accounted for by a factor he calls *social disorganization*, typified by such characteristics as a high birthrate, a high proportion of illegitimate children, a high TB rate and large numbers of neglected children; a lack of such disorganization was associated with high intelligence. Brightness in reading, on the other hand, was much more closely associated with an independent factor, labelled *maternal care,* indicated especially by a low infant mortality and a low incidence of infectious diseases.

In the second investigation, which took account of a larger number of variables, a different set of factors emerged. In particular, there were two different factors of parental care. The first, where psychological aspects of care – low birthrates, few children committed to public care, few children on probation – seemed most important, was associated with attainment in reading, but not arithmetic or intelligence. The second, where physical aspects of care seemed to predominate, was associated with a high incidence of brightness. A third factor, however, had high loadings on the ability and attainment measures, and low loadings on environmental variables.

Wiseman (1967) has also investigated the environmental correlates of attainment among ten year olds in Manchester primary schools. In this case the unit of analysis was the school and a stratified random sample of forty-four schools was chosen. In addition to seventeen home and neighbourhood variables included in the analysis, there were thirty-four school characteristics. As in the previous investigation, attainment measures were based on scores in objective tests. One factor accounted for 72 per cent of the variance in attainment; its highest loadings among environmental variables were for cleanliness of homes, number of verminous children, family crime record, proportion of children getting free school meals, appearance and sociability of children (a rating by the observer), socio-economic status and material adequacy of the home environment (a rating by the Welfare Department). Thus aspects of the home, rather than the school, environment were mostly closely related to attainment. The particular variables with high loadings on this factor suggest the importance of both *poverty* and *maternal care*.

With a subsample of the same pupils, factor analyses using the individual pupil as the unit inevitably brought into prominence a different set of predictors of attainment. Variables concerned with parental aspirations and literacy of the home had consistently high loadings on attainment factors. Peaker, too, had found these to be important for primary-school attainment, along with parental interest in the child's education. Wiseman's results with regard to parental interest are revealing: while 'having talks with teachers' and 'expressing a desire for a particular secondary school' were associated with high attainment, other indices of parental interest, such as 'complaints against teacher', 'discussed problem behaviour at school', 'belief that child is below standard' and 'belief that children should be brought on faster' had consistently negative loadings on attainment factors. It would seem from this that parental interest as such does not necessarily contribute to educational success; unless parents' interest involves support for the school and the teachers, it may well detract from their child's chances of success.

Wiseman (1968) himself emphasizes the findings of these several investigations that the environmental correlates of 'brightness' are not simply the opposite of the correlates of 'backwardness'. 'The factors associated with backwardness tend to be those denoting maternal attitude to the *child,* while for brightness the parents' attitude to *education* seems the more important.' Furthermore, environmental conditions appear to have more influence on whether a child is well above average in attainment than on whether he is well below average; it is the able child from an environment where education is not valued who is most affected.

While regression analysis and factor analysis have both helped to clarify the relation between environmental variables and attainment, they cannot answer the question 'Do variations in any specified aspect of the environment, acting independently of others, affect attainment?' Indeed, so long as one is dealing with a population in which many potentially influential variables are quite highly intercorrelated, this question cannot be answered merely by the choice of a suitable statistical technique. A partial solution may, however, be obtained if subpopulations can be defined in which the correlations between potentially important variables are low; then, for each subpopulation, it is more possible to distinguish the relation of each of these variables to success. Since virtually all the relevant variables appear to be correlated with social class, this is an obvious basis on which to subdivide a complete age-group.

Floud, Halsey and Martin (1957) used this approach in their study of grammar-school selection. Considering only working-class children, they compared the effects of material and attitudinal variations in home environments. Homes were classified as materially favourable or unfavourable on the basis of income, quality of housing, persons per room and amenities; and attitudinally favourable or unfavourable in terms of parents' aspirations for, and interest in, their child's education. Restricting the population to working-class children was effective in that there was only a negligible correlation between the two bases of classification. Results for grammar-school places are shown in Table 4; those for Middlesbrough exclude children from Roman Catholic families.

Table 4
Awards of Grammar-School Places to Working-Class Children from Different Types of Home (from Floud, Halsey and Martin, 1957, p. 108)

Home environment	Per cent awarded places in grammar schools	
	SW Hertfordshire (933 pupils)	Middlesbrough (774 pupils)
Wholly favourable	21	24
One aspect favourable only		
Material environment	9	12
Attitudes	23	15
Wholly unfavourable	6	5

When results for 'wholly favourable' environments are compared with those in which only parental attitudes were favourable, it is clear that the material environment of homes had a considerable effect in Middlesbrough, where the general standard was poorer, but none in south-west Hertfordshire. Thus material conditions may act as a threshold variable, being a serious handicap if below a certain level, but not having much influence if above that level. Once again the results suggest the crucial importance of parental attitudes for success.

Douglas (1964), in his longitudinal study of a national sample of British children, extended this approach of analyses within social classes. An analysis of variance tested the independent relation to attainment of four environmental variables, each apparently important. Separate analyses were made for boys and girls, for middle-class and manual working-class children, and for children aged eight and eleven. All four variables were found to be significantly related to attainment at both ages: parents' interest, housing (except for working-class girls), family size (except for middle-class girls) and the academic record of the school (except for working-class boys). Of the four, parents' interest (assessed by teachers' ratings and by visits to school) was most closely related to attainment and appeared increasingly influential as children grew older. The quality of housing appeared to increase in importance for working-class children with age, but to decrease in importance for middle-class children.

While these factors are thus independently associated with attainment, it must be remembered that they each tend to be associated with other possibly influential factors. For example, among the working-class families, the correlation between the parents' interest score and a maternal care score, obtained when the children were infants, was 0·48. It is useful to consider this result in relation to Wiseman's findings. In those investigations which took schools or wards as units rather than individual pupils, maternal care appeared as an important correlate of attainment; but in those studies, Wiseman had no measure of parental interest or encouragement. It is thus not possible to say whether maternal care in early childhood in itself influences attainment, or whether it is merely associated with other aspects of parental behaviour which *are* influential.

The close relationship between parental attitudes and success is equally apparent in the secondary school. In particular, parental attitudes appear to be of great importance in determining whether or not working-class children continue their education beyond the age of fifteen (Douglas, Ross and Simpson, 1968). For example, for those pupils who are from the most able third of the age-group and are from lower-working-class families, the proportion of those whose parents show high aspirations who stay on is over twice that for those with uninterested parents.

Douglas, Ross and Simpson (1968) made a particularly close study of the relation of attainment to family size and spacing, and birth order. Nisbet (1961) had suggested that the commonly reported negative correlation between family size and intelligence was partly due to the greater exposure to adult language enjoyed by children in smaller families. This hypothesis is supported by several findings from the longitudinal study. Differences related to family size were consistently greatest for vocabulary tests and least for tests of non-verbal intelligence. These differences did not increase, and for working-class children actually decreased, after the age of eight. Children two to four years different in age from their siblings had higher scores in attainment but not in non-verbal intelligence than those from families less widely (and also those more widely) spaced. Similarly eldest boys were superior to others in reading but not in non-verbal intelligence. And attainment was less related to family size among middle-class than among working-class children. All these results are consistent with the hypothesis that the relation of family size to intelligence and attainment is largely a function of the amount of time which children spend with their parents during early childhood. The interesting finding that boys with elder sisters had lower attainments than those with elder brothers may be explained on the same grounds, if it is assumed that girls are more often given child-minding duties.

There are clearly, however, other factors relating to family size and position which affect attainment. In particular, boys with younger siblings were more successful than boys who were only children. Not only were they superior in attainment, they also gained more grammar-school places and more GCE passes than could be predicted from this superiority, and stayed on longer at school.

Analysis of the correlates of attainment and success within each social class is not only valuable in that it makes it more possible to study the independent relation of different environmental variables to the criteria. It also reveals that the predictors of success are not always the same for each social class. Some differences of this sort have already been noted in Douglas's findings. Similarly Kellmer Pringle, Butler and Davis (1966) found that in social classes I and II, seven year olds who were not living with both their natural parents tended to be considerably poorer in reading ability than others; in social class III the tendency was not so clear; and in social classes IV and V it was not apparent at all. Swift (1967) emphasized this difference in 'symptoms' of success between social classes, and also demonstrated that correlates of success within the population as a whole may not be found when classes are considered separately. In a relatively small-scale and localized study, he found that scores on a general index of material prosperity, though closely related to eleven-plus success for his sample as a whole, were not related to success among either middle-class or working-class pupils. On specific items, however, differences emerged: home ownership was related to success among working-class families, as was *not* owning a car among middle-class families. Since it is hard to believe that ownership of houses or cars has a direct effect upon educational performance, these results may suggest different sorts of parental attitude conducive to success in the two social classes. A second index, of parental attitudes towards education, discriminated between the successful and others within the sample as a whole and also among working-class pupils considered separately, but not among middle-class pupils. Working-class children were more likely to be successful the more similar their parents' attitudes were to those of middle-class parents.

Up to this point we have considered several of the most carefully designed and most large-scale statistical surveys of home environment in its relation to academic success with the double aim of demonstrating the various approaches which have been adopted and of indicating the most substantial results which have been achieved. From these and similar investigations, one may abstract several aspects of home environment which have consistently been found to be related to attainment and success in school.

1. *Parental attitudes to education*, involving interest in school, encouragement to children, and aspirations for children's educational and occupational careers; such

attitudinal variables consistently emerge as being of outstanding importance.

2. *Educational level of the home*, involving the amount and nature of the formal education received by parents themselves, but also the cultural interests of parents and particularly the extent to which the reading of books is a normal activity in the home.

3. *Family size,* important in the years of early childhood, probably mainly in its effect upon the extent to which children spend time in conversation with adults; and, probably at least partly for the same reason, *birth order,* eldest children tending to be most successful.

4. *Quality of maternal care* of young children, which appears to be particularly related to the development of reading skills.

5. *Material prosperity of the home*, probably better thought of as *poverty*, since the evidence suggests that this factor is important only when income level, standards of housing, etc., fall below a certain level.

6. *Social disorganization,* involving a complex of neighbourhood phenomena, such as high illegitimacy rate, high birth rate, high incidence of crime, neglect of children, dirty homes and broken families. Like material prosperity, this factor is probably irrelevant to the great majority of children; but for children from 'problem families' and, more generally, from socially depressed areas of large cities, it appears to be of considerable importance.

7. *Abnormal family background*, in that one or both parents do not live with the child. Psychologically, this factor may be closely related to 'social disorganization', but whereas the latter refers to socially depressed neighbourhoods, individual children in all social classes may have 'abnormal' family backgrounds and, relative to others of the same class, it is middle-class children whose attainment is most affected by such backgrounds.

These general conclusions must, however, be qualified in various ways. The same features of the environment are not likely to be equally predictive of success for different subsections of the total child population. In different geographical regions, distinct subcultural groups and, as has been seen, in different social classes, the factors most related to success are likely to differ.

More fundamentally, the variables revealed as important by such statistical surveys are only correlates of success, or symptoms of the types of environment conducive to success or failure. They cannot be assumed to be causatively related to success, although in some cases it seems probable that this is the case. Nor can they be assumed to be independent of the many aspects of family life which, because they are so difficult to measure, have not generally been included for investigation in large-scale surveys. If these limitations are not taken seriously, one may be led to very debatable conclusions. Peaker (1967), for example, concluded, from his findings that 'parental attitudes' were highly correlated with attainment and were largely independent of 'home circumstances', that there was reason to believe that these attitudes might be changed by persuasion and that the attainments of children might thereby be improved. Yet even if one assumes that these attitudes themselves affect attainment, this optimism may well be unjustified; for although they may be relatively independent of material circumstances or parental education, the attitudes less conducive to success are likely to be an integral part of the whole pattern of living of many families: to alter them would then involve other fundamental changes, unlikely to result from mere persuasion.

The variables generally considered in statistical surveys are usually measured by ratings of home characteristics based upon visits to the home and interviews with parents. They cannot tell us much about the day-to-day behaviour of parents or about the processes whereby they influence their children; they give us a carefully chosen snapshot of the home environment, not a moving picture. Yet it is probably through social interaction with their children that parents most influence their success. In an American study, Dave (1963), working on this assumption, interviewed sixty mothers in an attempt to assess six different aspects of their behaviour which he hypothesized would influence their children's attainment. The over-all index based on measures of these six aspects correlated 0·80 with the general attainments of the children. This high correlation, though based on a relatively small sample, seems to confirm that it is the behaviour of parents which is influential and that the importance of the factors listed above is that they are symptomatic of differences in parental behaviour. In the following two sections we turn to the question of how different patterns of family behaviour influence children in ways which affect their academic success.

Personality characteristics, home background and
academic success

Which personality characteristics in children are most conducive to academic success? And in what ways, if at all, is the development of these characteristics the result of their parents' behaviour? Research aimed at answering this second question, by considering such specific aspects of behaviour as the types of punishment used or the degree to which mothers show affection for their children, has generally tended to be inconclusive. Not surprisingly, the effects of any one action, or even of a series of similar actions, seem to depend upon the general social psychological context in which these actions occur. For example, when a mother who is demonstratively affectionate towards her child slaps him and explains to him what he has done wrong, the effect is different from that achieved by the same action from a mother who tends to withhold her affection and who does not explain. Thus any generalizations which we can hope to discover are likely to be about general patterns of parent–child interaction and of family life as a whole. This leads to a third question: 'Can one identify several such general patterns of family life within a society?' This is a difficult task, especially in a complex and changing society such as modern Britain. Since every family is different, what one is looking for are ideal types, to each of which many families more or less conform; most families will show some characteristics of each of one's ideal types, and many will not be classifiable at all.

Probably the most fruitful attempts yet made at such general classification have been those using social class as a basic concept. A social-class system may be defined as 'a system of socially ranked groups, with varying degrees of social movement existing among them. Each group consists of people who participate, or may participate, in intimate social relations with each other, but who do not and may not associate freely with the group which are socially defined as "above" and "below" them' (A. Davis, 1948, p. 5). People who interact with one another regularly over a long period of time, and also live in similar material environments, tend to acquire similar values and patterns of behaviour. In any one community then, especially if it is relatively isolated, social class is likely to be a fairly reliable basis upon which to categorize patterns of family life. In a modern society, however, few communities are isolated and it is indeed only in the loosest sense of the word that we can talk of most people as living in communities. Furthermore, people of the same social class in different regions, or even different neighbourhoods within the same city, may well have their own distinctive ways of life. On a national basis, therefore, we cannot expect social class to be more than a crude indicator of family life. Both the value and the limitations of the concept of social class are apparent from Klein's (1965) ambitious attempt to synthesize evidence from anthropological studies of neighbourhoods in different parts of England, a study upon which we have relied heavily in the following pages.

In this section we shall examine the evidence about values, motives and other 'non-cognitive' personality characteristics which are associated, on the one hand, with educational success and, on the other, with family background. The following section will deal in a similar way with cognitive skills and particularly with language.

It is a simple and appealing hypothesis that the extent to which one cares about doing well on any tasks one undertakes is both a consequence of one's upbringing and an important determinant of one's success at school. Accordingly, the concept of achievement motivation – the drive to do well relative to some standard of excellence, merely for the sake of doing well (McClelland, Atkinson, Clark and Lowell, 1953) – has been the subject of widespread interest and intensive study. Among the characteristics found to be associated with high achievement motivation, assessed by responses to projective tests, have been a preference for moderately difficult tasks which present a challenge, with success or failure depending on the individual's efforts; a tendency to be relatively unaffected in performance by a lack of material rewards; and a readiness to deny oneself pleasures of the moment in order by one's efforts to achieve greater rewards in the future.

Motivation for high achievement is not, however, a unidimensional variable upon which people can be put into a single rank order. One distinction found to be necessary is between a conscious concern for achievement and an unconscious need for achievement (n-Ach). Thus projective test measurements have generally been found to bear little relationship to measurements of achievement motivation by self-report attitude scales. Mitchell (1961) factor analysed the scores of a sample of women college students on eight measures of achievement motivation and identified five different factors: (a) academic motivation and achievement; (b) self-satisfaction; (c) wish-fulfilment motivation; (d) non-academic achievement orientation; and (e) external (e.g. parental) pressure to achieve. The tests which had high loadings on the academic motivation factor were all self-report scales. As a result of these and similar findings, successful attempts have been made to develop measures of 'academic motivation' using inventories dealing with aspirations, attitudes to school and study habits. Entwistle (1968), for example, found that scores on his inventory correlated 0·41 and 0·50, for thirteen-year-old girls and boys respectively, with their teachers' estimates of attainment; and that the scale discriminated significantly between pupils who 'improved' and 'deteriorated' in their first year at secondary school.

The difference between self-report and projective test results is probably related to a conceptual distinction first made by B. C. Rosen (1956). He argued that achievement *motivation* – the drive to excel – should be distinguished from achievement *values,* and that achievement motivation will only lead to educational success and social mobility when associated with these values. He suggests three basic achievement-oriented values: a preference for attempting to actively manipulate one's environment to advantage, rather than passively accepting it; an individualistic orientation which allows a person to break his ties with primary social groups; and a preference for planning for, and deferring gratification until, the future. Subsequent research (e.g. Strodtbeck, 1958) has tended to confirm that holding these values is related to high attainment and even more to high educational aspirations.

Investigations of the relation of achievement motivation itself to attainment have produced inconsistent findings. Lavin (1965) found that of ten American studies using projective tests with college students, only four gave significant correlations with attainment. Achievement motivation has consistently been found to be correlated with IQ, and Bruckmann (1966) found that its relation to school stream in a sample of English primary-school children could be accounted for in terms of IQ. It is consistent with McClelland's theory that children with high IQs should as a result of their experiences of successful problem solving develop high n-Ach; but also that those with high n-Ach should, because of their concern to succeed in demanding tasks, develop higher IQs. Kagan and Moss (1959) found a positive correlation between n-Ach, assessed at age eight and a half, and increases in IQ between the ages of six and ten.

Lavin (1965) also summarized the results of investigations into the relation with attainment of several personality characteristics connected with achievement motivation. Characteristics which have with some consistency been found to be of value in predicting attainment include: the tendency to be independent or autonomous, to resist pressure to conform; impulse-control and persistence at tasks; and self-esteem and confidence in one's own abilities. In summary, although the evidence is not conclusive, it does seem that need for achievement, as measured by projective tests, and related characteristics are often conducive to educational success, though in what circumstances is not yet clear. Rosen's thesis that success is most likely when high n-Ach is associated with achievement-oriented values, while not yet established, is certainly consistent with the available evidence.

In view of findings that n-Ach is relatively stable from about the age of six, it is likely that the years of early childhood are particularly influential in its development. There is evidence that several different patterns of child rearing may be conducive to the development of achievement motivation. One pattern is that of rewarding children for their achievements and punishing them for their lack of achievement; several studies have demonstrated significant relationships between such parental behaviour and n-Ach. In a cross-cultural study based on an analysis of folktales, Child, Storm and Veroff (1958) found that, among societies using rigid, non-indulgent child-rearing practices, the rewarding of achievement and the punishment of its absence were highly correlated with indications of achievement motivation. But among societies in which child rearing was more indulgent there was no correlation between n-Ach and the use of rewards or punishments, and it was in these societies that achievement motivation tended to be highest; it therefore seems that other origins of achievement motivation need to be postulated. Argyle and Robinson (1962) hypothesized two such origins: that children might identify with, and attempt to emulate, achievement-oriented parents; and that where children have warm and dependent relationships with their parents, parental demands and exhortations for achievement may be internalized and applied by the child himself. The first of these hypotheses was only supported by their evidence from a questionnaire measure of achievement motivation; but on the second hypothesis, reported parental demands for achievement did tend to be correlated with scores on a projective test, and especially with the need to avoid failure. Other research, such as that of B. C. Rosen and D'Andrade (1959), indicates that high n-Ach develops when parents encourage independent achievement at an early age, set high standards of achievement for their children and show themselves to be emotionally involved in their children's efforts. Although parents of children with high n-Ach have been found to be fairly demanding, the wrong sort of demandingness – demands for achievements beyond the child's powers, demands for high standards in conformity behaviour, e.g. cleanliness, and demands made by dominating fathers – can inhibit the development of achievement motivation.

Achievement motivation has generally been found to be correlated with socio-economic status. Bruckmann (1966), however, found that the partial correlation when IQ was held constant was not statistically significant and, therefore, questioned the assumption that social class itself affected n-Ach. On the other hand, there is some evidence of relevant social-class differences in child-rearing practices. Klein (1965), reviewing the patchy and often impressionistic evidence available, concluded that traditional working-class mothers tended to be both more indulgent than middle-class mothers and also more punitive. It was in the consistency and deliberateness of parental discipline that she found the greatest social-class differences (cf. Newson and Newson, 1968), and she contrasts the 'arbitrary' socialization techniques most commonly found among working-class parents with the 'problem-solving' approach which was more common among middle-class parents. In middle-class families, the child is more likely to be taught to think of good behaviour as an achievement, resulting from his own understanding and impulse-control. Middle-class parents, too, when giving their children household chores to do, or when playing with them, tend to be more motivated by a concern that their children should learn to plan and to take pride in their independent achievements, and they tend to set higher standards of achievement and to supervise their children's activities more closely.

It is in the holding of achievement-oriented values that social-class differences appear to be greatest. Studies of traditional working-class neighbourhoods in England certainly suggest that the culturally dominant values have not tended to be conducive to educational success. In so far as such cultures *are* traditional, the individual is presented with little need or scope for major choices; instead he must learn the standards and roles which local convention decrees. Values need not be explicitly taught, nor need they be internalized; they are inherent in the pattern of community life, and conformity to them is achieved through the pressure of primary social groups. This is possible because of the existence of relatively stable closely knit social networks, of which extended families are an important part; and the importance which is attached to interdependence within the extended family, neighbourliness and solidarity with one's workmates makes individualist values inappropriate and unacceptable. Since any major changes in one's way of life, such as unemployment or ill-health, are likely to be caused by events outside one's control, planning for the future is futile: a short-term perspective and an almost fatalistic acceptance of most aspects of life are among the most frequently mentioned characteristics by observers of this type of working-class culture. And within the family, the possibility of different preferences leading to discussion and deliberate choice is greatly reduced by the traditional segregation between the roles and areas of responsibility of husband and wife.

In such communities, then, we seem to have the very

antithesis of those values which have been found to be associated with high attainment and aspirations. But this picture is based on accounts of those older working-class communities in England which have been studied; regional variations, and quite radical changes in recent years, due in part at least to greater material prosperity and large-scale rehousing, make it difficult to assess the extent to which this sort of cultural pattern exists today.

Prosperity makes choice possible and geographical movement tends to break up closely knit social networks. In a new environment, husbands and wives may become more dependent on one another's company, new possibilities may appear open to one and new reference groups may be adopted. Among attitudinal changes in recent years which Klein (1965) discerned among working-class families are: an increased awareness of the possibilities of choice, and a greater willingness to make decisions; a greater concern with the future, and with this a shift of emphasis within the family from the bread-winner to the child; more of a sense that one is responsible for one's own life, less reliance on luck; greater confidence in dealing with such institutions as schools or the civil service; less acceptance of one's social status as simply 'working class'; and a concern with such symbols of social status as home ownership. There appear to be considerable individual differences both among people in the older areas and among those on new estates in the extent to which such changes in attitude have occurred, but little is known about the causes of these differences. The effects of these changes, however, appear clear: the differences among working-class people, noted in the previous section, in their more specifically educational attitudes – encouragement of children, interest in school progress, educational aspirations – may be assumed to be closely related to these more fundamental differences; and it will be remembered that attainments were found to be closely related to these attitudes to education.

It cannot be overemphasized that the above statements about different patterns of life and child rearing among working-class families indicate general tendencies and trends, to which there are many exceptions, and are not such that they can be applied to any specific families. Similarly, while it is a fair generalization that middle-class people tend to hold values more conducive to academic success than do working-class people, it is also necessary to recognize the considerable diversity, in status, values and ways of life, that exists within the middle class. Here we shall consider only two 'ideal types' who may be thought of as representing extremes within the middle class in terms of both status and values, and also as manifesting two different ways of bringing children up to be educationally successful.

At one extreme is the traditional upper-middle class, of whom the majority of men are administrative and professional workers. The limited available evidence (cf. Klein, 1965) suggests that, along with economic security, people in this class also tend to enjoy psychological and social security, self-confidence and self-satisfaction. Thus although 'success' is valued, concern to be successful probably does not imply the same degree of stress as in other social classes. Most upper middle-class occupations involve a fairly high level of specialist expertise and within a man's own professional field he is generally independent and free from supervision. Independence, at work and in other contexts, is highly prized; and as this independence is expected, so it is assumed that one's behaviour will be dictated not by social pressures but by one's own internalized standards. Similarly one works hard primarily because the problems presented are inherently interesting and their solution a pleasurable activity. Life's goals are distant, general and abstract, and to achieve them requires thought, self-control and 'a sense of responsibility'. The rearing of children in this class tends to be careful and planned. Through firm and consistent discipline, values are internalized early. Throughout childhood all the main characteristics of training for achievement motivation are manifested, except perhaps in that parental affection is shown less through physical contact than in talking with the child. In particular, the child is taught to *enjoy* problem solving and learning, for example by the use of educational toys and language games, and by being encouraged to explore the complexities of his environment and to discuss them with his parents. In so far as the personalities of children of this class contribute to their educational success, the major factors are likely to be their easy conformity to the values of the school (which are similar to those of the home) and the confidence and relative pleasure with which they engage in school work.

We may contrast with these children some from families which in status are around the vague borderline between the middle and working classes, with fathers in low status white-collar supervisory or possibly skilled manual jobs. Several investigators have observed that the most successful children from this type of class background are those whose parents' social aspirations are well above their present or expected status. Swift (1964) found that middle-class children in one area were more likely to be selected for grammar school if their fathers were dissatisfied with their jobs and future prospects; and that this 'mobility pessimism' was found largely among the lower middle-class families. And Jackson and Marsden (1962) found that of the working-class children that they studied who successfully completed grammar-school courses, a very large proportion were from families which had close middle-class connections and parents who identified themselves with the middle class. Similarly, investigations in the United States have shown that working-class children are more likely to be successful if their parents belong to a 'sunken middle class' or are dissatisfied with the father's failure to 'get ahead'.

In all accounts of such families, an emphasis on educational qualifications is apparent; the qualifications, sometimes more than the education itself, are seen as necessary to achieve the clear goal of upward social mobility. From early schooldays, attempts are made to convince the child of the importance of education, and there is strong pressure on him to succeed. Klein (1965) suggested that these parents tend to be authoritarian, restrictive and over-protective, demanding conformity as well as achievement, showing affection sparingly and as a reward. In contrast to the upper-middle-class child, the child in this type of environment learns that achievement is desirable, not because completing the task successfully is inherently satisfying, but because it will win the parental approval and affection which cannot be assumed. Such a background seems unlikely to lead to the development of self-confidence or independence, but the evidence suggests that it often leads to considerable academic success.

We have indicated two very different types of middle-class home background from which children are likely to succeed at school. Most middle-class families probably show some features of each of these two extreme patterns. In so far as this is the case, they are clearly at an advantage over working-class families, at least those of the more traditional type; but how much of the differences in educational achievements between the two classes is accounted for by these differences in values and child-rearing practices we cannot tell.

Language, home background and academic success

Although it is cognitive characteristics of personality which are most directly and obviously related to educational success, there is comparatively little detailed evidence about the influence of family environment on aspects of cognitive development. Before school age, the extent to which children have experiences which are helpful for cognitive development and, therefore, their readiness for school when they start, depends very much on their parents. In recent years this has become widely recognized, with the consequence, for example, that American concern with the educational disadvantages of the 'culturally deprived' has been concentrated on the pre-school years. But whatever the specific nature of these disadvantages may be, the home environment is unlikely to change dramatically when the child does start to attend school; so that any attempts by the school to overcome initial disadvantages will not normally be reinforced, and may well be counteracted, by the child's continuing experiences at home. More generally, the more the nature of the cognitive activity engaged in by the child and his parents at home differs from that normally required at school, the more of a hindrance to educational success the home background may be hypothesized to be.

There is probably little significant variation among the home environments of children in most Western societies with regard to many kinds of experience necessary for cognitive development. There is no evidence, for example, that the sensory experience of children from different social classes varies in any relevant way. One way in which children's learning environments *do* vary significantly is in their social relationships and particularly in the nature and extent of their language experience. There is considerable evidence (cf. Lawton, 1968) of social-class differences in the language behaviour and skills of children. The tendency for middle-class children to have superior linguistic competence, observable from as early as eighteen months, appears to increase with age. Scores on vocabulary tests have been found to be highly correlated with social class, as have measures of the 'normal' speech of children, such as sentence length. Several investigations (e.g. Loban, 1963) have found that with children above the age of about seven, social-class differences are most apparent in the complexity of sentence structure, for example in the use of the more difficult types of subordinate clauses and of second-order subordination. Other evidence indicates that the more abstract the language required, the greater the relative difficulty experienced by working-class children.

Language plays a crucial part in the development of children's learning and thinking. Being able to attach verbal labels to objects helps the child to remember them, to classify them and to discriminate between them. He can learn to perceive general relationships more easily if he can use such expressions as 'bigger than' or 'on top of', or on a more advanced level 'or'. Through language, he can organize his experience and direct his own actions; it helps him to think in terms of possibilities, to develop a time perspective and generally to become less tied to his immediate experiences. Language has been found to be particularly valuable in that it helps the individual to manipulate and reorganize a situation mentally when attempting to solve a problem; people with limited language skills have been found to be relatively inflexible and dogmatic in their thinking.

Evidence of the importance of language for educational attainment is seen in findings that deaf children (much more than blind children, for example) tend to suffer considerable educational retardation. Also, the best predictor of academic attainment in secondary schools has generally been found to be verbal-reasoning ability, with ability in language usage and interpretation almost equally effective. In general, the more success depends on abstract thinking and symbolism, the greater the influence of language is likely to be.

It thus seems likely that language differences contribute to social-class differences in educational attainment. There is little direct evidence of this, but it has usually been observed that school entrants from homes of low socioeconomic status tend to be more retarded in language development than in other respects. And Bereiter and Engelmann (1966) cited evidence which indicates that social-class differences in ability are much smaller for deaf children than for hearing children, suggesting that these differences depend to a considerable extent upon language experience.

The importance of language in the relation between social class and educational success had been the major theme of the important theory developed by Bernstein (1961, 1965). Bernstein suggested that the linguistic differences which have been found between social classes reflects two quite different modes of speech which are typical of lower-working-class and middle-class people. These modes of speech are both a consequence of the different types of social relationship and the different values dominant in the life of the two classes, and are also a major factor in perpetuating and reinforcing these differences.

Two types of language are suggested: elaborated code, or formal language, in which the individual's precise and particular meaning is made explicit by the use of the formal possibilities of sentence organization; and restricted code, or public language, characterized by very little deliberate personal choice of syntax, so that the meaning is not made explicit or precise. Restricted code speech is asserted to be used in any social context where identification with others, as opposed to individual differentiation, is stressed. In such a context, communication about the day-to-day concerns of the group is possible without the elaboration of meaning; and to use language of which the meaning is implicit and understood because of the conventions of the group helps to maintain the solidarity of the group. Thus restricted code speech is found in all social classes; but whereas lower-working-class children learn only this mode of speech, middle-class children also learn to use elaborated code speech in those contexts where it is necessary.

Bernstein relates differences in language to features of traditional working-class and upper-middle-class cultures mentioned in the previous section. Fundamental to the distinction between the two speech codes is the difference between the 'affective inclusiveness' characteristic of the closely knit working-class community and the middle-class emphasis on the distinctive thoughts and feelings of the individual. The greater time perspective of the middle class, their greater emphasis on decision making and planning, and their problem-solving approach to life all lead to a need for language which is precise, finely differentiated and abstract. In rearing children, their concern with motives and with the justification of their judgements in terms of consistent values and goals requires the verbalization of feeling and explicitness about intentions and purposes. The tendency of working-class parents, on the other hand, to stress conformity and the effects of behaviour, and to base their authority on their position alone, is compatible with the non-verbal expression of feelings and a language usage involving relatively concrete symbolism. Bernstein emphasizes the middle-class concern with self-control, rather than social control, and that 'the process of subordinating behaviour to verbally elaborated meanings will progressively become the major instrument by which the growing child becomes self-regulating'.

Working-class children learn restricted code language partly because this is the model with which their parents provide them. This is reinforced, however, by the greater amount of time which working-class children tend to spend with one another and not with their parents; the children's or adolescents' gang is just the type of social group for which restricted code speech is most appropriate.

What distinguishes those limited to a restricted code is not so much a poor vocabulary as their lack of ability in using language to organize their experience. Their language is more suited to communication about things than about processes, ideas or relationships. Research (e.g. Lawton, 1968) has tended to confirm that the specific differences between the two codes described by Bernstein are found when upper-middle-class and working-class language is compared. Irrespective of intelligence, adolescents from independent fee-paying schools used relatively more subordinate clauses, and especially more complex forms of subordination, more passive verbs, more varied adjectives, adverbs and conjunctions, and said 'I think' more often, in group discussions than did secondary-modern schoolboys; the latter used more personal pronouns and more 'socio-centric' phrases (e.g. 'Wouldn't it', 'You see'). Similar differences are also found between the essays or informal letters of the two classes. Lawton, however, found that working-class boys, when faced with questions 'demanding' abstract replies, could, with difficulty, use lan-

guage of a much more elaborated code type than they
normally did. In the same way, Newson and Newson (1968)
found working-class mothers well able to communicate
their thoughts and feelings in an interview situation, although when speaking to their children they rarely used
anything other than restricted code speech. The Newsons
suggest that working-class speech patterns should not be
explained in terms of any lack of skill, but in terms of attitudes, emotions and contexts.

To be limited to restricted code speech affects the working-class child's chances of educational success in several
ways:

1. It reinforces in him such cultural values as living in the
   moment, accepting life as it comes, and lack of indivi-
   dualism or individuality.

2. Because of the restricted code of his parents he is less
   likely than a middle-class child to receive answers to
   questions at home, and any answer received is likely to
   contain less information of a less accurate nature
   (Robinson and Rackstraw, 1967); as a result he will be
   less well informed and become less curious.

3. At school, he is not likely to be amenable to the un-
   emotional speech and carefully discriminating language
   which the teacher uses to control behaviour; 'I'd rather
   you made less noise' will contain no imperative to him.

4. More generally, much of what the teacher says is likely
   to be incomprehensible, dependent as it is upon discrimination between different adjectives, conjunctions
   or types of subordinate clause. The child may realize he
   does not understand, or he may 'translate' the teacher's
   language into his own and assume that she is stating the
   obvious and repeating herself. He is likely to become
   increasingly inattentive to what she says.

5. Most important are the implications for the child's cognitive development. Bernstein (1961, p.302) summarized
   these as follows: 'It is suggested that a correlate of this

linguistic form is a relatively low level of conceptualization, an orientation to a low order of causality, a dis-
interest in processes, a preference to be aroused by, and
respond to, that which is immediately given, rather than
to the implications of a matrix of relationships.'

Bernstein suggests that the restricted code user is likely
to find most difficulty with those aspects of the curriculum
and those teaching methods which are most dependent on
insightful generalization, abstraction and the active exploration of relationships. Because his language emphasizes
the concrete and the arbitrary, he will experience less difficulty with associative or 'drill' learning – a kind of learning increasingly discouraged. Recent evidence obtained by
Jensen and his colleagues in California (Jensen, 1969) was
consistent with this hypothesis: social-class differences in
ability have been found to be large and consistent in tasks
involving conceptual learning and problem solving, but
non-existent in tasks involving associative learning. Furthermore, the two types of ability are highly correlated
among middle-class children, but much less so among children of low socio-economic status; among them, high ability in associative learning appears to be a necessary but
not a sufficient condition for high ability in conceptual
learning. According to Bernstein's theory, this is because
the limitations of a working-class child's language, even
when he is of high ability, are likely to make it difficult for
him to think on an abstract level.

In many respects, Bernstein's theory is as yet unsupported by empirical evidence. We cannot be sure that linguistic
differences are as influential as he suggests; and there is
very little detailed evidence about the relation of language
usage either to personal interaction and values in the home,
or to behaviour and learning difficulties at school. From
the theoretical viewpoint, it is in some respects rather vague
and, largely because of this, has met with criticisms from
both sociologists and linguists. None the less it appears to
be consistent with most of the relevant available evidence;

and it is the most far-reaching attempt yet made to explain and to relate many of the processes whereby working-class children are less likely to achieve educational success.

Demographic variables other than social class

While the major environmental correlates of educational success within the population of Britain are those associated with social class, there are other differences in home background which may influence success. Some of these are considered briefly below.

Urban–rural differences. In recent years it has consistently been found that the attainments of children from rural backgrounds tend to be substantially inferior to those of urban children. Barr (1959), reviewing this research, concluded that although this poorer performance may be partly due to selective migration of the most able families and to inferior formal education in rural areas, it can be almost entirely accounted for in terms of social class, since a larger proportion of the rural population are manual workers. This, however, does not necessarily provide an *explanation* of rural–urban differences in attainment. Since there are obviously many differences between town and country in the way in which most manual workers live, it may well be that different factors account for their relatively low attainments; for example, the particularly low incomes of agricultural workers may make material conditions and economic considerations more important in rural areas.

Research in the United States has indicated that pupils from homes in large metropolitan areas, like those from rural areas, tend to have lower achievements than others; and in one investigation, Rogoff (1961) showed that both the attainments and the educational aspirations of high-school students from small towns and from the central areas of large cities were lower than those of students *of the same intelligence and socio-economic status* from suburban areas or large towns. Before the causes of such differences are understood, much more research will be required.

Bilingualism. There are several different circumstances in which a child may have to be bilingual. Only one language may be spoken at home, while another is used at school and in almost every other context: this situation most commonly occurs in the case of recent immigrants to a country. At the other extreme, the language of school instruction may rarely be required outside school, a situation in which many Irish children find themselves. Or both languages may be used at home, in school and in the community at large. In attempting to generalize about the effects of bilingualism on educational success, it is necessary to take account of such variations in the extent to which, and the contexts where, each language is used.

Macnamara (1966), surveying many studies from all parts of the world, concluded that, despite the poor design of most investigations, the mass of evidence showed fairly conclusively that bilinguals are generally inferior to monoglots in their linguistic skills, but that no conclusion was possible about the specific causes of this relative retardation. Bilingualism, the evidence also indicated, hampers a child's progress in problem, but not mechanical, arithmetic, presumably because the former, like most school subjects, involves considerable use of language. Macnamara himself found 'native-speakers of English in Ireland who have spent 42 per cent of their school time learning Irish' to be, when in the fifth standard class, approximately seventeen months of 'English age' behind British children, sixteen months of 'Irish age' behind native-speakers of Irish; and, if they had been taught arithmetic in Irish, to be eleven months of 'problem arithmetic age' behind British children.

The two main groups of native British children whose home language is not English are those whose parents speak Welsh or Gaelic. Welsh research on bilingualism was summarized by Jones (1966). In none of this research have socio-economic and urban–rural differences been adequately controlled, so that findings, for example, that children from Welsh-speaking homes tend to be inferior in both verbal and non-verbal intelligence must be interpreted with considerable caution. However, even when differences in non-verbal intelligence have been allowed for, children whose only home language is Welsh have consistently been found to be markedly inferior in English attainment to native-speakers of English; but those whose parents speak both Welsh and English have generally been found to be only slightly inferior. On the other hand, this latter group tend to be low in Welsh attainment. It has been found that, where only Welsh is spoken in the home, the child is likely to live in a Welsh-speaking community; but where parents speak both languages, it is more likely that English will predominate in the community as a whole.

Vernon (1969) made a detailed study of twenty 'representative' boys from predominantly Gaelic-speaking homes and twenty from predominantly English-speaking homes in and around Stornoway, the main town of Lewis in the Outer Hebrides. On attainment tests he found no significant differences between the two groups or between them and national norms, but the Gaelic-speaking group were below average on some tests of conceptual development and of English oral comprehension. Vernon points out that other investigators have found that the attainments of children from more isolated Gaelic-speaking communities in Lewis compare less favourably with national norms.

Although the Welsh and Scottish evidence is far from conclusive, it does seem to be no great disadvantage for a child to speak a second language, provided he has ample opportunity outside school to use the language in which most school teaching is conducted. Not surprisingly, he is unlikely to achieve the standard in both his languages which monoglot children achieve in their one. And if he does not use the language of the school elsewhere, he is likely to be seriously educationally retarded.

Immigrants. In recent years, immigrants to Britain have come mainly from Commonwealth countries, especially the

West Indies, India and Pakistan. Reviewing publications on the educational problems and potential of the children of these immigrants, Goldman and Taylor (1966) commented that 'those which can be classified as research, in the rigorous sense of the word, are very few indeed'. From the accounts of teachers and other observers, however, it is possible to identify several factors which are likely to put these children at a disadvantage in comparison with native British children.

With regard to the material conditions of their homes and the extent of formal education received by their parents, two factors already shown to be potentially influential, most immigrant children are among the worst placed children in Britain. For most Asian children, the fact that English is not the language spoken in their homes is an obvious and major disadvantage. Less obvious is the considerable disadvantage suffered by West Indians as a result of the limitations of the Creole form of English spoken in most of their homes. Associated with language differences are cultural differences. The more different the culture of their society of origin is from that of Britain, and especially that of British schools, the less support parents will be able to give children in their life and work at school. In addition, the pattern of family life to which they are accustomed, such as the authoritarian, matriarchal and father-absent pattern commonly found in the West Indies, may not be conducive to educational success.

Social attitudes to racial differences may also affect children's success in a number of ways. Because of stereotyped beliefs about black children, teachers or others may discriminate against them, for example in streaming, in secondary-school selection or in not encouraging them to have high aspirations. Because children may learn from the behaviour of others to think of themselves as inferior, they may become less motivated to succeed. If they perceive society as rejecting them, they may reject the 'success' values of that society. And, if children believe that their race is discriminated against in entry to high-status occupations, they may limit their aspirations accordingly. All these phenomena have been found to affect black children in the United States (Ausubel and Ausubel, 1963). There is no evidence about the extent to which they influence the attainments of non-white children in Britain.

In spite of these many potential disadvantages, the evidence about the attainments of immigrants, at least at the primary-school level, is encouraging. The Inner London Education Authority (1967a) surveyed the attainments of immigrants transferring to secondary education from all junior schools where immigrants accounted for at least one-third of the roll. The children were classified as West Indians (590), Indians and Pakistanis (74), Cypriots (237) and others (150). The mean attainment of each group was well below that of all ILEA children, the West Indian group being weakest especially in mathematics; but of the 71 per cent of the total sample who were classified as not requiring further special instruction in English speaking, only the West Indians were much below average. Attainment was found to be highly correlated with length of residence in England, and those who had had a complete primary-school course in England did not differ significantly in attainment from the complete age-group. Furthermore, among those who had received four or more years of English primary education, there were no significant differences between the four immigrant groups. In view of this, the investigators suggest that the poorer attainments of more recent West Indian immigrants may be due, not to inferior home environments when they are settled in Britain, but to the stress caused by separation from parents and reuniting after several years. Among West Indians, but not among immigrants from the Commonwealth countries, it appears to be a common practice to leave children at home and then to send for them when the parents are established in Britain.

Ashby, Morrison and Butcher (1970), in a study of Asian immigrants in Glasgow, also found that attainment was closely related to the length of time since arriving in Britain.

Fifty-nine children of immigrants were compared with their 150 Scottish classmates in the last two years of five primary schools. While those immigrants who had been in Britain less than four years were significantly inferior to the Scots on all tests of attainment and intelligence, those who had spent nine or more years in Britain did not differ significantly from the Scots on any test except arithmetic, on which they were *superior*. The medium-stay (four to eight years) group were inferior to the Scots on the intelligence tests but not significantly different on any of the attainment tests.

In both London and Glasgow, immigrant children, though given special instruction in English language where necessary, are educated in the same primary-school classes as native children. Given these conditions and a full primary education, it appears that the obvious disadvantages suffered by these children are fully compensated for by less obvious advantages, most likely more parental encouragement and greater achievement-orientation than is common among working-class families in central urban districts. It is also worthy of note that the attainments of the native children in the London schools studied were not significantly different from those of the age-group as a whole. Considering the districts in which these children lived, their attainments certainly do not appear to have been depressed by the presence of immigrant children in their classes.

The older children are when they immigrate to Britain, the greater the disadvantages they face. It seems clear that lack of mastery of the English language is a major factor in this. Another factor, revealed by the Glasgow study, is the extent to which parents become involved in and familiar with the host culture. Ratings of homes with regard to this were positively correlated with ability and attainment scores, being higher for girls than for boys and particularly high for the medium-stay groups. The attitude of immigrant parents to the host culture thus appears to have considerable influence on the extent to which their children overcome their initial disadvantages.

Conclusion

However much importance one attaches to genetic factors, the evidence that has been reviewed demonstrates that the homes in which British children grow up have a great influence on their academic success. Furthermore, as a result of statistical, psychological and anthropological research, we are able to say a good deal about the sorts of homes which are relatively likely to provide a basis for academic success, and about the sorts of homes which are not. To go beyond this, to substantiate hypothetical explanations of how environmental factors affect cognitive development, aspirations and success is likely to prove much more difficult. It is indeed an impossible task with the research techniques which have been used in Britain up to the present time.

A stage has been reached where it would be most fruitful to carry out controlled experiments to test such hypotheses by implementing programmes of action based upon them, and assessing the effects which these programmes have upon pupils' attainments and success. Although many innovations in the past have been aimed at enabling pupils to achieve greater success, only rarely have these innovations been implemented in such a way that their effectiveness could be judged. It is more difficult, however, to decide upon the sort of innovations that are most likely to overcome the handicaps that have been revealed; in particular, would it be necessary to attempt the immense and morally debatable task of changing patterns of home and community life in predetermined ways? Or can the desired goals be achieved more easily by making the schools more adaptable to the needs of children from different home environments? We return to this question at the end of this chapter.

The school environment

It has consistently been found that differences in attainment among British children are much less closely related to their school than to their home environments. Similarly, in the United States, 'when socio-economic factors are statistically controlled, it appears that differences between schools account for only a small fraction of differences in pupil achievement' (Coleman *et al.*, 1966, p.21). None the less, the influence of school variables is far from negligible; Peaker (1967), for example, found that 17 per cent of the variation in attainment among English primary-school children could best be accounted for in terms of school variables. And, since teachers and educational administrators can modify school environments more readily than they can affect the homes of pupils, the effects of variations between schools may be of particular interest.

Educational success depends upon access to education. In England and Wales the major variation in access to education has been in the different proportions of pupils for whom different local education authorities provide courses which can lead to academic qualifications. In 1961 this corresponded closely to the proportion in each area attending grammar schools. The Committee on Higher Education (*Robbins Report*, 1963) found that the correlation of the percentage of pupils in each area allocated to grammar schools with the proportion in the area still at school at age seventeen was 0·82, and the correlation with the proportion who entered higher education was 0·71. These close relationships could only partly be accounted for by the social-class compositions of different areas. Douglas, Ross and Simpson (1968) found that the effect on success of differences in the provision of grammar-school places was greatest for working-class pupils, especially girls.

Instead of academic courses being provided for a limited number of pupils in selective schools, pupils of all abilities may be admitted to comprehensive secondary schools. What effect this has upon the proportion who are successful on any criterion is, of course, a source of heated political debate, but whether it is a fruitful question for educational researchers to ask is doubtful. For one thing, it is difficult to find a definition of comprehensive education which is sufficiently precise for research purposes and at the same time sufficiently relevant to the practical situation for research to be possible. Secondly, the effects of factors such as the age and size of schools and the attitudes, qualifications and experience of teachers are in practice difficult to distinguish from the effects of the 'comprehensiveness' of schools. Finally there is so much scope for variations in the internal organization and policies of comprehensive schools that the probability of any general conclusions about them must be small.

The most thorough investigation yet of comprehensive education (Svensson, 1962) involved a complete year-group of Stockholm children who were separated into different courses at different schools when aged either eleven, thirteen or fifteen. The attainments of the more able pupils were not affected by the age at which they were selected, but less able pupils scored better if they had been to the more comprehensive schools. In the very different social and educational conditions of Britain, however, the same may not apply. There are some indications that in Britain, more pupils achieve success in external examinations at comprehensive schools and, more definitely, that pupils tend to stay longer at school; but generalization is dangerous. What can be said with confidence is that many pupils achieve a success that would have been virtually impossible for them in a selective secondary school system (e.g. Inner London Education Authority, 1967b), and that in *some* comprehensive schools the number of pupils achieving success in external examinations is greater than would have been possible in most selective systems.

Pupils may be segregated into different schools on the basis of other characteristics than ability. For example, throughout Britain most children from Roman Catholic families are educated in Roman Catholic schools; because this segregation is so general, there can be no evidence about its effects upon attainment or success. Another common basis for segregation is sex. As with comprehensive and selective schools, it is difficult to compare the attainments of pupils at single-sex and co-educational schools. Single-sex schools tend to be older, more traditional, larger and more often in urban districts; even when consideration is limited to state schools, the socio-economic status of single-sex-school pupils tends to be higher; and teachers in the two types of school tend to differ in their educational attitudes. None the less the weight of evidence suggests that after other factors have been taken into account, boys do better in co-educational schools; the same appears to be true for girls so far as mathematics is concerned but in other subjects no general pattern is discernible (Dale, 1968). There is, however, evidence (e.g. Douglas, Ross and Simpson, 1968) that pupils at co-educational schools tend to leave school earlier.

The basis upon which schools select their pupils is only one of the ways in which they may affect their pupils' success. Douglas (1964) has demonstrated the importance of differences between primary schools in their record of achieving grammar-school places. He showed that, except for working-class boys, this variable was significantly related to average score on his tests at age eight even when the effects of pupils' social class, family size, housing and parental interest were allowed for. It was also significantly related to changes in test scores between the ages of eight and eleven, and by the age of eleven it was second only, among the variables he considered, to parental interest in its power to predict the ability of pupils. Furthermore, if a child's school had a good record of achieving grammar-school places, his chance of getting such a place himself was 20 per cent higher than his test scores at eleven seemed to warrant.

Some schools, then, are consistently more effective than others in helping their pupils to achieve success. What are the distinctive characteristics of such schools? This question has been explored by the use of the same sort of multivariate techniques as have been applied to home backgrounds. One general conclusion which emerges from such studies is that the most influential aspects of schools are not their physical characteristics, the facilities they provide, nor even their curricula, but rather the characteristics of the people within the schools, both pupils and teachers. Thus Kemp (1955), in one of the earliest investigations of this type, found that the 'morale' of the school, judged from the behaviour of the pupils, was, apart from socio-economic status of the school district, more closely related to attainment than any of his other variables. Peaker (1967) found that the school variables which added most to the power of home variables to predict attainment were various characteristics of the teaching staff, particularly the length of their teaching experience and their teaching marks when students. One of the most thorough and extensive of such investigations has been that of Coleman *et al.* (1966) in the United States. Three groups of variables were considered: school facilities and curriculum (e.g. library and laboratory facilities, comprehensiveness of the curriculum, use of ability grouping); teacher characteristics; and the background and aspirations of pupils. Apart from the effects of their own home backgrounds, pupils' attainments were found to be most related to the characteristics of fellow-pupils, with teacher characteristics almost equally important. Both student body and teacher characteristics were found to be particularly influential among the more socially disadvantaged groups. Important teacher characteristics were their own educational backgrounds, their teaching experience, their scores on a test of verbal ability and, negatively, their preference for teaching middle-class pupils. Coleman pointed out, however, that many teacher characteristics were not considered, so that these results do not necessarily indicate which aspects of teachers' behaviour are of greatest influence. And, although Kemp (1955) and Warburton (1964) found small positive correlations between attainment and the 'progressiveness' of teaching, it is clear that questions about the nature of effective teaching and effective teachers are much too complex to be answered at this broad level. What *is* clear is that the quality of the teaching staff is much more important than are other aspects of educational provision within a school. A further factor, not revealed by these general studies of the school environment, but significantly related to pupil attainment (Gross and Herriott, 1965) is the quality of the professional leadership given by headmasters to their staff.

Of other school characteristics studied, among those most often found to be related to attainment are class size and school size: the larger the class, and the larger the school, the higher pupils' attainments tend to be. The latter is readily explained in terms of the reduced ability of small schools to provide a range of educational experiences comparable with those of larger schools. Coleman, in fact, demonstrated that when the availability of various specific facilities was taken into account, the remaining relationship between school size and attainment was negligible. Similarly the relation of class size to attainment can be explained in terms of the poorer performance for other reasons of pupils in rural schools and depopulated central urban districts. But in view of the considerable importance which teachers often place on reducing class sizes, the absence of evidence that smaller classes are associated with superior attainment is interesting. It may be that teachers tend to use the same teaching methods irrespective of class size; or that, if they do adapt their methods according to the sizes of their classes, they tend to be less skilled in the methods which they use for smaller classes.

One of the features of schools which has attracted most interest and research is policy with regard to the grouping of pupils into classes, and particularly the effects upon attainment of grouping according to ability. Despite innumerable investigations, no clear statement can yet be made about the relative merits of ability grouping (streaming), random grouping or grouping in other ways. One common finding (e.g. Svensson, 1962) is that while streaming has no effect on the attainments of more able pupils, it tends to lower the attainments of the less able. But some studies (e.g. Barker Lunn, 1970) have found no consistent differences in attainment between streamed and unstreamed schools for pupils of any level of ability. Another common, but not universal finding is that streaming tends to be 'self-confirming'. Douglas (1964), for example, found that over a three-year period the relative attainments of children in upper streams improved, while those of children in lower streams deteriorated; these trends were most marked among the least able pupils in the upper streams and the most able in the lower streams.

Most research on streaming has ignored teacher characteristics and patterns of teaching in streamed and unstreamed classes. Two recent investigations, however, have focused attention upon the behaviour of teachers. Among the findings of an extensive and carefully designed study in New York (Goldberg, Passow and Justman, 1966) were that the attainments of other pupils in arithmetic tended to be higher when there were pupils of below average ability in the class; and that when there were very able pupils in the class, the attainments of others tended to be higher in science and in social studies. The investigators suggest that the explanation of these results is that teachers emphasize different subjects when faced with classes of different ability composition; for example, when there are less able pupils in the class, 'basic' subjects are emphasized. Barker Lunn (1970) found that teachers in streamed and non-streamed schools tended to favour the grouping system they were working with and that preferences for streaming or non-streaming were associated with differences in a wide range of educational attitudes and teaching behaviours, those favouring non-streaming being generally more 'progressive'. However, even when interactions between grouping polices and differences in teachers' general attitudes were considered, no systematic differences in pupil attainment emerged.

It seems probable that ability grouping in itself need not have any effect upon attainment. The ability composition of classes, however, can influence attainment indirectly through its effect upon teachers' expectations of pupils and perceptions of what subjects and standards are appropriate for them. The ability composition of the classes which a teacher is accustomed to teach may also have an effect upon his general educational attitudes. Furthermore, there are indications that teaching skills are important: ability grouping can only be of value if teachers are sufficiently skilled to capitalize upon advantages resulting from a limited range of ability in their classes; conversely, teachers trained to teach or experienced in teaching classes which are relatively homogeneous in ability may lack skills which are necessary when the range of ability is greater. But ability grouping, as well as influencing teachers, can affect the self-perceptions of pupils and also the nature of informal social groups among pupils, making it more probable that the composition of these groups will be closely related to academic attainments.

The influence of peer groups

Although it is well established that informal social groups influence the behaviours of their members, there is little evidence of the effects which they have upon attainment and educational success. One reason for this is the difficulty of distinguishing peer-group from other influences. Among the major factors determining the membership of informal groups among children and adolescents are the nearness of their homes, whether they are in the same school class and, especially among older adolescents, the similarity of their interests and attitudes. And since peer groups tend to influence their members most in those matters about which there is greatest consensus among them, their effect upon academic achievement tends to be largely in reinforcing the influence of other significant aspects of the social environment.

There is, however, some evidence that peer groups do exert an independent influence upon success. As already noted, Coleman *et al.* (1966), in their national study in the United States, found that student body characteristics were more closely related to attainment than were any other school characteristics. Variations between schools in the educational level of students' home backgrounds were highly correlated with their educational aspirations. But, whereas in the southern states home background was the more influential characteristic, in the northern states aspirations of the student body were more important. As might be expected, it was· at the high-school rather than the primary-school stage that attainment was most related to the characteristics of other students. This influence was much the least among those racial groups of highest average attainment; confirming, Coleman suggests, that students with home backgrounds conducive to achievement are less susceptible to other social influences. In this study, it should be noted, students' attainments were related to characteristics of the whole student body. If, instead, characteristics of the informal groups of which students were members had been considered, it seems probable that the correlations with attainment would have been higher. In a study of one American high school, Herriott (1963) found that the expectations of 'best friends' accounted for more of the variation in students' aspirations than even the expectations of their parents.

One of the clearest demonstrations of the influence which social interaction among students can have is given by Wallace's (1966) study of students in their first year at an American college. When they first arrived at university, students were very concerned to achieve good marks, but seven months later their aspirations in this direction had been greatly reduced, becoming more like those of most students in the upper classes. This change, however, was not uniform. The more contact a first-year student had had with students in upper classes, the lower the aspirations of the students with whom he had been in contact, and the greater his need for acceptance by others, then the more, in general, he had lowered his aspirations. Group influence thus appears to depend upon the extent to which a student is involved in a group, upon the norms of the group and upon his own personality.

In this college there was clearly a dominant student sub-culture in which little value was placed upon academic achievement. Other studies have found that various types of subculture tend to be dominant in different colleges, though in larger colleges and universities several such sub-cultures may co-exist in some strength, often being centred on different departments or faculties. Coleman (1960), who has emphasized how different the values of adolescent sub-cultures are from those of the dominant middle-class adult culture, found that among the students in some American high schools high status could be achieved through athletic prowess and success in other extra-curricular activities, but not through academic success. The influence of the student social system was shown in that correlation between in-telligence and attainment in these schools was significantly less than in schools where status was associated with scholarship, many of the more intelligent students having relatively low attainment. The norms of the high-status groups not only did not encourage high academic achieve-ment; they seemed to be effectively opposed to it.

It is questionable whether peer groups in Britain have as much influence on educational aspirations and achieve-ment as they appear to have in the United States. In most British research, the membership and values of peer groups have been found to be closely related to social class and to the ability grouping which plays a much bigger part in British than American schools. Furthermore, as Sugarman (1967) suggested, few British schools offer adolescents the sort of extra-curricular pursuits common in American high schools which allow the development of a social system identified with the school but none the less opposed to 'official' adult values. In his own research, in boys' secon-dary schools in London, Sugarman found a negative cor-relation between commitment to the 'teenager' role – pop music, teenage fashions, coffee bars, dating and smoking – and commitment to the 'pupil' role, signified by the desire to be a good scholar. Teenage commitment was negatively correlated, at a highly significant level, with attainment and also with attitudes to school, with orientation towards the future and with teachers' ratings of general conduct. These results do not necessarily indicate any influence of adolescent groups, especially since teenage commitment was also found to be negatively correlated with the 'intellectual quality' of home backgrounds. Together with other research, however, it suggests that in many British secondary schools there are two types of adolescent sub-culture, one largely identified with the values of middle-class adult culture and most confidently upheld by pupils from middle-class homes, the other a hedonistic 'youth culture' which rejects the values of the school and which mostly involves pupils from lower-middle-class and working-class homes. In so far as pupils are free to choose their own associates they can, therefore, find group support either for high educational aspirations and attainment or for a refusal to accept the demands of teachers.

Hargreaves (1967) in his detailed study of a boys' secondary-modern school, found evidence of two such clearly differentiated subcultures. But the anti-school sub-culture, in this working-class district of a northern city, did not appear to grow out of a positive attraction towards a national teenage culture. Concentrated in the lower streams of the school, it appeared rather to represent a reaction of these pupils to their experiences in school, with their formally low status being aggravated by the behaviour towards them of pupils in upper streams and of teachers; its norms are indicated by Hargreave's label, 'delinquescent'. Although to some extent related to home backgrounds, the two subcultures appeared to be progressively differentiated during the four years of secondary education, the streaming system being a major factor in this process. By the third and fourth years, peer-group norms in the upper streams supported the teachers' values and in these classes there were positive correlations between attainment and informal status. Boys in the lower streams, however, had very little opportunity to interact with those in upper streams, and were under strong pressures from their classmates to inhibit any desire for academic achievement.

If, however, the values of adolescent groups in schools are classified only in terms of their support for the school and academic values, important variations may be missed. Jackson and Marsden (1962), for example, mentioned a grammar-school group who rejected most of the school's values – pride in the school, exclusiveness, decorum, 'leadership', etc. – but were concerned about learning and their school work. Only fifteen working-class pupils opposed to the grammar-school ethos had been found who successfully completed an A-level course in any of several years' intake to four grammar schools; and ten of these fifteen belonged to one group of friends in one school. Jackson and Marsden suggested that many of the working-class pupils admitted to these grammar schools had similar attitudes, but being isolated, found the atmosphere of school so hostile that they left early. These ten were fortunate in that they were contemporaries and acquainted; they appeared to owe their success very largely to the support of the group.

The home and the school

We have emphasized the separate effects of variations in home and school environments upon success, and have found that the former are much the more important. It remains to be asked, however, whether the academic success a person achieves may not be due more to the suitability of the 'match' between his home and school environments than to the characteristics of either considered in isolation from the other. In particular, do the school experiences of working-class children complement what they have learned at home as appropriately as do those of middle-class children?

There are, in fact, several specific ways in which the relative disadvantages of children from working-class backgrounds may be seen to be increased because of their experiences of school:

Inequalities of provision. Because the schools and houses

of a district were usually built at much the same time, children from central urban districts tend to attend schools with the worst buildings and facilities. This in itself may not have much effect upon their success, but because of the schools, the district and the children themselves, teachers are not attracted to these schools. Those who are employed in them tend to be the least experienced and to obtain transfers to 'better' areas as soon as possible. Among schools in American cities, Herriott and St John (1966) found a positive correlation between the average socio-economic status of pupils and the professional competence of teachers, their interest in pupils, their readiness to make innovations and their cooperation with other school staff. And, as noted earlier, it is among such schools that the influence of teachers upon attainment appears to be greatest.

Parental interest. We have seen that the interest which parents take in their children's education is closely related to their chances of success. Although it is not yet clear why parental interest is so important, in so far as parents' knowledge about what happens in school, their involvement in decisions about their children's educational careers, and communication between them and teachers are relevant factors, working-class families tend to be at a disadvantage. There is ample evidence that the majority of teachers and headmasters are unenthusiastic about contact with parents. And, as Jackson and Marsden (1962) for example, have shown, most working-class parents are much less ready than middle-class parents to demand that they be kept informed or that notice be taken of their views. Lack of social confidence in the school context, belief that 'the school knows best' and ignorance about the educational system combine to make it unusual for them to take the initiative in communication with the school. In an experiment in one working-class primary school (Young and McGeeney, 1968), various efforts were made by the school to increase parent–teacher contact; significant increases in attainment occurred, though it was not possible to determine whether these were due to the experimental innovations. In general it seems likely that if schools gave parents more encouragement to participate in their children's education, 'lack of parental interest' would be a serious handicap to a much smaller proportion of pupils.

The values of the school. Reference has been made at several points to the conflict between the values upheld by the school and those of many children and adolescents, especially those from working-class backgrounds. To some extent this appears to be outside the control of the schools; achievement-oriented values are probably necessary for success. But there is no evidence that many values held by schools, such as conformity with conventional middle-class standards of dress and conduct, loyalty to the school, or the need for pupils to conform to the 'child' role in their relations with teachers, are related to attainment. And it is demands such as these, rather than a lack of concern for school work, which lead many adolescents into bad relations with their teachers and to early leaving.

Teachers' expectations and judgements. Teachers, like others, tend to have stereotyped views about children from different social classes. Because of this, they tend to expect less of working-class pupils, to assess their abilities as lower than they are and to have less ambitious goals for them. These tendencies are perhaps most clearly seen with regard to the streaming of pupils. Douglas (1964) found that more working-class children were placed in lower streams in primary schools than would have been predicted from their measured abilities. Once they have been placed in streams, the different attitudes and goals of teachers lead to increases in the existing differences in attainment between social classes. Streaming also increases the correlation between social class and attainment by fostering peer groups within, rather than across, social classes. But while the tendency for teachers to promote the fulfilment of their own expectations can most easily be demonstrated in the use and effects of streaming, teachers' differential behaviour towards pupils from different social backgrounds within their classrooms is also likely to be a powerful factor contributing to the relative lack of academic success achieved by working-class pupils. Rist (1970), for example, in a three-year observational study of one class in an American elementary school, found that within their first fortnight in school the middle-class children in the class came to be perceived by the teacher as the most able and the most enthusiastic; and that, thereafter, teachers concentrated their efforts on helping these children. Other less direct evidence suggests that such teacher behaviour may be widespread.

In these various ways, school environments tend to put working-class pupils at a disadvantage. On the other hand, there is no evidence of ways in which school environments tend to be particularly helpful to working-class pupils. In recent years, however, considerable efforts have been made, especially in the United States, to identify methods whereby the school system can compensate for the 'cultural deprivation' experienced by 'disadvantaged' children in their homes. Most of these efforts have been concentrated on the pre-school age-group, with the intention of allowing children from underprivileged homes the chance to start school on equal terms with middle-class children.

Many different types of programmes have been developed in the United States to provide such compensatory education, although few of them have been planned in such a way that their precise characteristics could be specified or their effectiveness reliably assessed. Some projects, including those of the federally financed Project Head Start, have attempted to influence all aspects of children's development; but while in other respects apparently very successful (e.g. with regard to medical care), Head Start programmes appear to bring about only a slight and temporary improvement in most children's cognitive skills (Cicirelli *et al.*,

1969). Other programmes have been based on the argument that since the school is attempting, within a relatively short time, to compensate for disadvantages which children have experienced over several years, the only way to bring these children to the same level of readiness for school as middle-class children is to concentrate all available resources upon essential cognitive skills. Thus Bereiter and Engelmann (1966), for example, in one of the most successful pro-grammes to be evaluated, have given concentrated instruc-tion and practice in the minimum essentials of language thought to be necessary for learning at school. Even those children participating in the most effective programmes, however, have tended to fall increasingly behind national attainment norms during their first three years at school. This has led to demands for the extension of compensatory programmes into the school years, and also for programmes beginning earlier in childhood, extending into children's homes with such objectives as teaching mothers how to speak to their children.

The idea of compensatory education implies that the children for whom it is intended, and the homes from which they come, are in some way deficient. Now it is true that the performance of working-class children on tests of ability and 'readiness' does tend to be inferior to that of middle-class children; but, it may be argued, this is because working-class cultures are different from the culture of the middle class and of the schools, so that the cognitive attain-ments of working-class children are not properly reflected in their scores on school tests. On such grounds, Baratz and Baratz (1970) argue that compensatory education for chil-dren from working-class black communities is bound to fail, since efforts to compensate for deficiencies are in reality attempts to supplant one culture for another, and also that, in its devaluation of Negro culture, compensatory education is a form of institutional racism.

Bernstein (1970) rejects the concept of compensatory education for similar reasons; but he makes explicit the problem that, while working-class culture may be viewed as different but not inferior, middle-class socialization does more to promote those skills towards the achievement of which formal education is and must be directed. Whereas middle-class children tend to be 'oriented towards receiving and offering universalistic meanings *in certain contexts*', working-class children more often tend to be 'oriented towards particularistic meanings' (Bernstein, 1970, p. 117); yet 'the introduction of the child to universalistic meanings of public forms of thought is not compensatory education: *it is education*' (p. 120). Thus the process of education is likely to be more difficult for working-class than for middle-class children. This difficulty is greatly increased, however, by the failure of schools to observe the fundamental principle that we should work with what the child can offer. Both the normal practice of schools and the concept of compensatory education devalue those very experiences which teachers must utilize if working-class children are to be effectively educated. For

if the contexts of learning – the examples, the reading books – are not contexts which are triggers for the child's imaginings, are not triggers on the child's curiosity and explorations in his family and community, then the child is not at home in the educational world. ... If the culture of the teacher is to become part of the consciousness of the child, then the culture of the child must first be in the consciousness of the teacher (Bernstein, 1970, p. 120).

Such principles, in our opinion, indicate the most effective means whereby working-class children can be enabled to achieve greater academic success. It seems unlikely that much progress could be made in attempting radically to alter parents' behaviour towards their children; nor is much permanent gain likely to result from adding extra instruction, however carefully planned, to an educational programme which is basically designed for middle-class children. It is rather in the day-to-day work of primary and secondary schools that changes must be made. From our understanding of the ways in which children's home environments vary and of the educational disadvantages currently experienced by working-class children, it should be possible to devise contexts for learning which are sufficiently flexible for all children from all types of social background to be able to build in school upon what they learn in the context of their homes. It is through the assessment and progressive improvement of school environments planned on this basis that we are most likely to increase our understanding of the social factors which influence academic success and also make such success possible for more people.

2 Social Behaviour and Education

Some of the most striking developments of the school years concern the social behaviour and personal values of pupils. New skills are acquired in the handling of everyday relationships with others, characteristic modes of conduct develop, systems of personal values are formed and personal identities become more clearly differentiated.

Many agencies contribute to the shaping of the short-term and persisting social characteristics of our pupils. In the early years the family is the most potent source of influences, but once children have entered school new opportunities are created for adults and for peers and older pupils to influence individual development. Certainly, formal education seems well placed to have marked social effects. It has, in the first place, broad, if rather ill-defined social objectives, expressed, for example, in such terms as 'moral education' or 'training for citizenship'; and secondly, it is able by its organization to focus the attentions of a few salient individuals, teachers especially, upon concentrations of children.

But, what effects do our schools have? Are they major sources of effective influence, or are other agencies, such as home and peer group, of over-riding importance? And, if schools have influence with some or most of their pupils, in what ways is it shown and how is it achieved?

Social behaviour is such a complicated and extensive subject that a selection of topics is essential. In this chapter five aspects are discussed: experimental work on social influence, the development of 'morality', interaction in small groups, perceptions of self and others, and studies of educational influences. The first four topics do not deal directly with schools and teachers; their prime purposes are to illustrate some of the general processes at work in influence and interaction, and to indicate where these processes operate. By taking this approach it is hoped that educational influence will be seen in its wider context, and that general findings can be brought to bear on the particular situations of the classroom and school. The final section then picks up particular studies within the school context itself.

Processes of influences and interaction: experimental studies of performance and learning

How do individuals seek to influence one another's behaviour? Two of the simplest instances are where a single individual is joined by another or where two or more work side by side upon the same tasks. In both cases the subject's behaviour is very likely to change; he will cease some activities, he will begin others, and where he is working at a task the rate of performance will change. Apparently mere presence or common activity are alone sufficient to produce changes in behaviour. However, a distinction has to be made between subjects who are performing well-established and familiar activities and those who are acquiring skills. Presence and co-action generally facilitate performance, that is, the production of previously learned responses; they often impair the acquisition of novel ones.

Reinforcement

Presence and co-action, then, are not sufficient in themselves for learning to take place. The next step is to shift attention from the physical encounter onto the characteristics of those who are involved and, in particular, to assume that every individual seeks to satisfy personal needs and to reduce discomforting states. On this basis, social influence upon learning and performance is contingent upon the ways in which one individual manipulates reinforcements rewarding or punitive, to another.

A half-century of experimental work has produced an

enormous and controversial literature on learning, and a great deal is now known about the role of reinforcers, especially those that satisfy biological needs such as hunger and sex, in controlling behaviour. Most experiments have used laboratory animals so that generalizations to human learning have to be made cautiously; moreover, many human needs arise from our social experiences and may or may not be derivations of the more basic biological ones studied in animals. Nevertheless, this work has direct theoretical and practical relevance to human behaviour.

Social reinforcers, that is, those under the control of others, are of many kinds – expressions of approval and praise, head nods, smiles, verbalizations like 'yes' or 'uh-huh', physical-verbal demonstrations of affection, and the granting of access to resources. They can be highly specific bits of behaviour, applied in an effortless and hardly noticeable way; on the other hand, they may consist of more general behaviour patterns incorporating many elements. They can be applied by single individuals, such as a parent or teacher, but equally can stem from a group such as a child's peers in the street or the classroom. Also, they can affect learning or regulation of performance over a wide spectrum of behaviour – verbal responses, physical activities, expressions of feelings and opinions.

In one investigation of the effects of social reinforcers upon verbal behaviour (Centers, 1963), students, ostensibly waiting for an experimenter to collect them for a laboratory study, were individually engaged in casual conversation by a confederate of the experimenter. He manipulated various simple reinforcers during each conversation. Analysis of the recorded conversations showed that total verbalization, output of informative statements and numbers of opinion statements were effectively controlled by the confederate, all showing significant increases when reinforcement was given and decreases when it was withdrawn. In a study of opinion expression, Singer (1961) showed that simple acknowledgement of 'good' and 'right' led to increased expression of pro-democratic and anti-authoritarian opinions. Not only, then, can the amount of what an individual will say be affected, but also what he will say. Other illustrations of the effects of social reinforcers are given later in the sections on parental behaviour and on the teacher's power in the classroom.

These studies are uncomplicated by many of the factors present in natural encounters, where the child or adult may well have established affectional relationships with the person who controls the reinforcement, where two or more individuals may be providing different sanctions to foster particular behaviours, or where comparably effective reinforcers are used to enhance conflicting responses. Complications also arise over determining the more effective patterns of reinforcement, especially where practical situations impose constraints upon parents, teachers and others who seek to influence.

Caution has to be shown when attempting to make generalizations about social reinforcement – with the added danger that when they are made they can seem as little more than trite observations. However, two broad ones are worth making since they suggest valuable orientations to the treatment of children. Drawing upon experiments on learning, Broadbent (1964) suggests that the most effective pattern of reinforcement for children would be (a) to emphasize the particular behaviour that is wanted and to praise or approve on every instance it appears, (b) once the connection is established between the behaviour and the reward, to reward on infrequent and irregular occasions, and (c) when doing so over the long term, to make the frequency of the reward contingent upon the frequency of further appearance of the behaviour. The second generalization from experimental work concerns the relative effects of praise and blame upon learning: here the findings from a large number of studies reviewed by Kennedy and Willcutt (1964) are that praise commonly facilitates learning whilst blame often has depressing effects.

Children in particular are exposed to highly salient individuals who are in powerful positions to reward or punish them. Are some likely to be more effective reinforcers than others? Stevenson, Keen and Knights (1963) compared the performance of infants on a game when parents and strangers provided reinforcers like 'That's very good.' With these children the strangers produced a significantly greater increase in response rates. Lacking other evidence, however, it is not possible to say how far this is typical. Bandura, Ross and Ross (1963) examined theoretical predictions about children's behaviour when exposed to adults who were either 'controllers' of resources valued by the children, or were 'consumers', the resources in question being attractive toys. Here, the children were more likely to be influenced by a power figure (a controller of resources) than by one whom they presumably envied because he was a consumer of things they desired. Children seem to be more attracted by the prospect of mastery over events than by merely being allowed to participate in them.

Imitation of models

Whilst both the power and relevance of social reinforcement can be demonstrated readily, it may not be a necessary factor and is certainly not a sufficient one for explaining learning or performance in children. Children are in continual contact with adults. These adults, with some of whom they have particularly close relations and lengthy periods of intensive exposure, have well established repertoires of socially appropriate and effective behaviour. Children can readily observe what they do and say and how they express their feelings. It is not necessary, then, for children to acquire ways of behaving through trying one behaviour after another until they hit upon the appropriate ones, nor perhaps for them to get there by being told what is expected, then being reinforced until the required responses are dominant. Short cuts are available through behaving approximately as the adults do (and, of course, as older children or attractive peers do).

In the subsequent discussion the term 'model' will be used to represent the individual who can be observed;

'imitation' will be used to describe the process in which observation of the model's behaviour or expressions affects the observer so that subsequent behaviour becomes more similar.

Both social reinforcement and the provision of models who exhibit the desired behaviour can be effective in controlling children's responses. In practice, of course, they often complement one another; the parent or teacher does or says the appropriate action, thought or opinion, then expresses approval when it appears in the child's behaviour. Because of this, it is not easy to determine from observation what their relative efficacy is. However, an ingenious experiment by Bandura and McDonald (1963) demonstrated that the provision of a model can be the over-riding factor. Five- to eleven-year-old children who exhibited two distinctive forms of moral judgements were assigned to one or other of three experimental situations. One group observed adult models who expressed moral judgements counter to those of one group, and the children were reinforced with verbal approval for adopting the models' judgements; a second group observed the models but did not receive reinforcement for adopting the models' behaviour; the third group had no adult models, but children were reinforced whenever they expressed judgements contrary to those they had intended to exhibit. In the first two of these situations, major changes in moral judgements were produced, and these changes persisted after the experiment. However, little change took place in the third situation, where no model was present. In providing a demonstration, the model greatly facilitates the acquisition of the approved response. He can equally establish a disapproved one, sometimes unwittingly, by acting himself in a manner contrary to the behaviour he would approve of in the child!

Personal characteristics of both models and observers can affect the extent of imitation and the persistence of the acquired behaviour. Imitation can increase where the model is rewarded, where it is the more dominant parent and where it has high social status. However, there is no consistent evidence on the other variables which might seem to be of likely importance such as the degree of realism of the model (whether 'live' or filmed), affective relations between model and observer, and sex of the model. Little evidence is available on the characteristics of the observers. Studies often reveal no differences between the sexes, but a fairly consistent finding is that boys imitate more than girls where the model is displaying aggressive behaviour. Emotional states and personal traits are associated with imitation: more imitation is found where observers are angry, high in authoritarianism, generally 'cooperative' or high in dependence.

One study is worth specific mention because it brings together three important issues: film influences, imitative aggression, and the retention of modelled behaviour. Hicks (1965) arranged for children of four to six years of age to view male or female adult and peer models presented on film. Six months after seeing the films the children were re-observed in order to assess the long-term influence of the models. It was found that the male peer had the most immediate influence in shaping children's aggressive behaviours while the adult male had the most lasting effect. Also, a significantly greater number of the models' behaviours were recalled after six months than were performed. Commenting upon the results, Hicks notes their particular 'importance in light of the frequency with which aggressive adult males are presented in movies and television'.

Moral development

Some of the most absorbing manifestations of social influence are found in those situations in which adults seek by one means or another to foster moral conduct and values in young children. For the most part theories and research on moral development have dealt with the infant and pre-school child, and with the behaviour of parents. However, they do have a great deal of relevance to educational practice, for from an appreciation of the rearing practices of parents and from information on the moral characteristics of children from different social backgrounds and at different stages of development teachers are better able to estimate the possible range and extent of their influences upon pupils and to recognize some of the probable effects of different patterns of personal conduct.

Conscience and self-control

Several theories have been put forward in order to represent what it is that a child acquires as a basis for moral conduct, and to explain the processes of acquisition. Psychoanalytic theories (see Freud, 1923; 1932) offer some of the most elaborate accounts, hinged upon three central concepts – superego, guilt and identification. In these accounts, the basis for moral conduct is the superego, an internal mechanism which once installed in the child then regulates conduct in an autonomous and consistent manner over time and different situations. The superego is thought of as a guilt mechanism which inhibits socially unacceptable impulses, particularly those of a sexual or aggressive nature, by producing or threatening the child with emotional discomfort. Thus the prime motive for acting morally is the self-punishment that would arise from moral transgressions. This punitive view of morality has a parallel in the explanation of how the mechanism itself is installed: guilt reactions in the child are the outcome of identification processes in which he models his behaviour upon his parent in order both to maintain a warm and nurturant relationship, and to resolve anxieties and fears arising from rivalries over affection between himself and his parents.

Other explanations of the acquisition of self-control come from the experimental psychology of learning (see Eysenck, 1960). These are commonly formulated in ways which are more readily open to empirical testing than is the case of psychoanalytic interpretations, much less emphasis is placed upon the idea of some internal regulator of conduct, and there is more concern with observable parental

techniques and their effects upon children than with sym-
bolic accounts of parent–child conflict. In some respects
they resemble popular conceptions of morality as something
based upon a persistent training in 'good' habits. However, the notion of generality of moral conduct, implied by
such terms as conscience or superego, is used, and identification (often called imitation) remains to explain and describe the transmission of parental conduct and values.
Furthermore, most learning theory accounts base the
primary acquisition of moral conduct upon anxiety, fear
or guilt, so that inhibition and avoidance characterize the
child's motivation; there is little reference to a morality of
considered judgement, conscious choice or altruism.

Although the various theories have many important differences they are largely in agreement on two matters of
interest to teachers: (a) that many of the basic moral
characteristics of children are established prior to formal
schooling, and (b) that the prime factors involved in the initial shaping of children's characteristics are the patterns
of reinforcements employed by parents, and the kinds of
exemplary models to which children are exposed.

Since some of these views on the acquisition of morality
lay stress on the early years, they may appear to have rather
depressing implications for educationists. However, in
principle at least this need not be so. There is sufficient
evidence from other fields of child development to show
that intellectual skills are vastly increased between infancy
and adolescence. Kohlberg (1966) is now the major ex-
ponent of views about the development of moral knowledge and judgement which indicate the changing cognitive
skills of schoolchildren. His work not only shows the importance of the school years, but also the need to integrate
the influences of early 'conscience' training with the child's
increasing intellectual grasp of a social order in which it
lives. Secondly, widening social involvement after infancy,
coupled with growing intellectual sophistication, can create
the conditions for children and adolescents to develop a
morality which rests increasingly upon self-interpretation,

a more rational analysis of issues, and decision making in complex situations where early acquired precepts and conventional habits may be of limited relevance and value.

The possibilities for school influence will be discussed later. At this stage it is more appropriate to sketch in the background to moral education by considering first some of the evidence on the rearing techniques employed by parents, and then some of the moral characteristics of children.

Child-rearing techniques

Although many reports on the rearing techniques employed by parents already exist, the on-going survey of a large sample of parents and their children which is being conducted by the Newsons (1968) is of particular interest because of its thoroughness and the information it provides on current behaviours of English parents and children from various social backgrounds. Several references will be made to their studies, the first concerning parents' views on their responsibilities in training their children.

When the mothers of four year olds were interviewed they proved highly articulate and widely concerned about their responsibilities and methods of rearing. Their most immediate concern was to train their children in specific social habits – arbitrary conventions differing between families and social backgrounds. However, beyond this, maternal practices and expectations focused upon the inculcation of desirable character traits which would result in more generalized behaviour – truthfulness, confession of wrong-doing and the use of apology. It was at this level that their most sophisticated intentions, reflecting a shift from arbitrary social convention and habit formation, were apparent, for through repeated verbalization and the use of themselves as exemplars, they sought to establish broad principles which could be regarded as characteristic of 'moral' rather than 'conventional' thought and behaviour. Thus, the dimly comprehending infant was exposed to notions and practices of reasoned arbitration and regard for the rights of others and responsibility towards them, and to subtle ideas on reciprocity, equity and obligation.

Given, however, that parents have many and often sophisticated intentions, what do these mean in terms of their actual patterns of rearing and their effects on children? One approach has been to try to derive broad distinctions between types of rearing techniques, identifying in the process the major characteristics of each, then to investigate associations between a particular technique and the behaviour of children who experience it. One such common distinction is that between 'psychological' methods – that is, discipline based upon reasoning with the child, punishment in the form of some withdrawal of affection, and display of affection for approved behaviour – and those parental techniques which rely more upon physical punishment, non-reasoning demands for conformity and deprivation of desired resources. Many studies have now been done on this basis, and a common finding is that moral behaviour in children, whether assessed in terms of resistance to cheating, signs of guilt, low anti-social aggression or use of confession, is stronger where parents tend to use the 'psychological' techniques and where there is little recourse to physical punishment (e.g. Bandura and Walters, 1959; M. Hoffman, 1963). However, the effectiveness of 'psychological' methods seems to be bound up, on one hand, with parental warmth towards the child, and on the other, with parental consistency and demands for high standards (Glueck and Glueck, 1950).

Such effectiveness is not surprising. In the first place, since one basis for regulating the child's conduct lies in parental affection, with disapproval being shown by its withdrawal and approval by expressions of warmth, these techniques get at the child's dependence upon the salient persons in his life. It is a far more alarming threat for the child to be deprived of affection and nurture than for it to receive relatively minor, if frequent, physical punishment. Equally important factors in its effectiveness are the physical and verbal modelling elements. Parents are more likely to present themselves as non-aggressive models. Where they are actually or are perceived to be physically violent and hostile themselves their children can acquire the same behaviour – the parents are effective demonstrations of the viability of undesirable behaviour (Bandura and Walters, 1959). Verbal behaviour apparently or actually indicative of satisfactory moral standards, such as confession, apology and self-criticism, may also result from the modelling effects of 'psychological' discipline. Since parents who use these techniques place some stress on the verbalization of 'proper' behaviour, their children gain experience in verbal expression. A possible illustration of this appears in the Newsons' survey (1968) where, although neither they nor the parents expected any immediate moral pay-off from the rearing techniques used with the four year olds, there appeared nevertheless highly significant differences in the use of confession by children, depending on whether or not parents themselves placed much expectation on their children admitting to transgressions and they themselves used apology for transgressions against the children.

Considerable differences in typical rearing techniques are found for parents from various social backgrounds. Frequency and content of verbal interaction are considerably different, with middle-class parents generally interacting more, through songs, story telling and explanations to their children, encouraging them to talk on family occasions such as mealtimes, and showing greater readiness to speak to their children on a wide range of intimate matters such as sex. Their children are, for example, less likely to be discouraged from talking on such occasions as mealtimes but, more important, words are more often seen as agents of truth than as means of evasion of issues. Truth distortion, for example, is much more often used by mothers in unskilled workers' families – 'Don't bite your nails, there's a beetle under them', 'This lady's come to take you to prison' or 'I'll put you in a home.' Furthermore, middle-class parents show a preference for reasoning with children, for explaining why they expect obedience, for self-confession to children, and for intervening in and encouraging child arbitration in peer and sibling disputes rather than encouraging the child to hit back.

Investigations of rearing techniques in different social contexts have helped enormously in identifying the real life characteristics of social influence in the infant years. The continuation of longitudinal studies, such as the Newsons' work, is necessary in order to describe the interplay of parent and child in their various backgrounds, and its relation to school factors over the period of formal education.

Some moral characteristics of children

Whilst it would be quite beyond the purposes of this chapter to review the extensive work on children's moral characteristics there are some aspects of moral development which should be mentioned because they have a particular bearing upon the school years and upon the possibilities open to teachers to influence pupils.

Consistency and stability of characteristics. When children are observed cheating, behaving in hostile ways or helping others, can any predictions be made about their behaviour from one situation to another? Can we expect that the child who is resistant to forms of temptation or who acts dishonestly will show these characteristics later in life? How consistent and stable are their characteristics?

A factor analysis carried out on data obtained in Hartshorne and May's classic investigation of moral traits (1928–30) did indicate a small general factor running through experimental measures of children's cheating (Burton, 1963), but the weight of evidence on honesty, self-sacrifice to the group or charitable ends, and self-control, is clearly in favour of specific situational conduct in children, influenced by expectations of punishment, the probability of being found out and the rewarding consequences of the situation.

Stability over time is a complex matter, often difficult to investigate and requiring extensive longitudinal study. Mac-Farlane, Allen and Honzig (1954) reported little evidence for the stability of behaviour traits over the pre-school years. Use of confession increases with age (Maccoby and Whiting, 1960), and the same holds for various expressions of guilt (see Aronfreed, 1961).

Another way of looking at questions of consistency and stability is in terms of associations between distinctive modes of moral expression – conduct, feelings and judgements. For example, does the child who is moral in the sense that he expresses guilt over transgressions also conduct himself morally? Some studies have shown considerable consistency over modes; substantial correlations have been obtained between measures of moral knowledge and experimental measures of character traits, and between knowledge and ratings of 'good character' made by children's peers and teachers (Hartshorne and May, 1928–30). Amount of confession in young children has been found to be associated with later resistance to cheating, and Kohlberg (1963) has reported significant correlations between maturity of moral judgement and assessments by ratings and tests of 'conscience', 'fairness with peers' and cheating. Self-blame and confession are also associated with socially conforming behaviour. Against these findings, little association has been reported either between strength of stated belief in 'virtues' and ratings of character, or between resistance to cheating and stated unwillingness to cheat.

Clearly, whichever way one looks at these matters only a limited amount of stability and consistency can be demonstrated. The different modes of morality appear to develop largely independently of one another and do so at different rates and with different degrees of susceptibility to background and situational influences at different periods in children's lives. This being so, there would seem to be extensive opportunities for persons other than parents to exert considerable influence in the post-infant years upon aspects of child morality – although it is certainly not clear as to what aspects are most open to such influence, nor which techniques are most likely to be effective.

Cognitive characteristics. Most of the research on children's acquisition of morality and subsequent development has dealt with conduct, moral traits and feelings, and rather less attention has been given to cognitive 'skills', although these would seem to have particular interest to teachers because of their close concern with fostering intellectual development in many spheres. Among such 'skills', which we can assume are open both to broad developmental modification as children grow up and to social influence, are modes of moral judgement, ability to de-centre or take the role of another, general intelligence, ability to control impulses and to defer gratification, skills in assessing factors in particular situations and in anticipating events, and capacity to maintain focused attention on matters. These represent in various ways a coolly rational basis for morality – or for prudent social action.

Both ratings and experimental measures indicate that the more intelligent tend to display a more sophisticated level of moral judgement. Also, as judged upon measures of cheating, they may be more honest. However, it has to be remembered that high performance on tests of intelligence usually reflects superior verbal skill, that bright children probably have less cause to cheat in many situations and that they are more likely to be skilful in avoiding detection. Kellmer Pringle and Edwards (1964) have demonstrated other associations with intelligence. On tests of 'moral wickedness' and 'moral incidents' given to pupils of high, average and low ability, they found that those of low ability cited fewer wicked actions, their thinking was less abstract in dealing with moral incidents, they tended to assign blame in transgression situations according, for example, to the amount stolen rather than in terms of intentions of the stealer, and they were less punitive and more willing to give an offender a second chance than were the more able children. Ability to defer immediate small reward for a larger reward in the future has been studied by Mischel (1963) who found that this characteristic discriminated between relative cheaters and non-cheaters. Several studies of delinquents have pointed to differences between them and non-delinquent children and adolescents in ability to focus attention and to control impulses. However, little seems to be known about the social and physiological factors involved in these differences.

The most coherent body of evidence on cognitive characteristics deals with the nature and changes of moral judgements in childhood and adolescence. This work is a particular facet of widespread study in many 'subject' areas, such as science, history and religion, which seeks to describe and classify ways of thinking, and which has already had important effects upon curriculum design. In the moral field some of the earliest studies were done by Piaget (1932), based, for example, upon observations of children in game situations and the recording of their beliefs about rules, or upon children's responses to transgression incidents. More recently, Kohlberg (1963) has extended the techniques of questioning subjects on their judgements of the rightness or wrongness of individuals' actions, and on their reasons for such judgements, to include sophisticated moral dilemmas which make demands across the whole school age range of pupils. With different age groups up to sixteen years he claims to have established three distinctive levels in the development of moral judgements:

Level I. Pre-moral
    Type 1. Punishment and obedience orientation
    Type 2. Naïve instrumental hedonism

Level II. Morality of conventional role conformity
    Type 3. Good-boy morality of maintaining good relations and the approval of others.
    Type 4. Authority maintaining morality.

Level III. Morality of self-accepted moral principles
    Type 5. Morality of contract, of individual rights and of democratically accepted law.
    Type 6. Morality of individual principles of conscience.

Classificatory studies of this kind have sometimes been too rigidly interpreted in terms of unitary, generalized stages of development. However, they are chiefly of interest in other ways: as a valuable exercise in describing the complexities of judgemental behaviour, in pointing to the intellectual processes involved in attaining something that might reasonably be described as 'conscience', and in bringing together, in ways which are of particular interest to teachers, psychological work on the development of morality and philosophical views on maturity of moral judgement and conduct.

Sex differences. Sex differences in moral characteristics are of considerable theoretical and practical interest. At the theoretical level, psycho-analytic approaches have suggested that girls would have weaker consciences than boys, whilst social-learning theories have predicted either little difference between the sexes or a balance in favour of girls. At the practical level, accounts of sex similarities and differences are relevant to expectations about the moral development of boys and girls, and in turn to the appropriateness and effectiveness of different forms of social influence.

Results are now fairly well established on a number of issues. Girls have a lower incidence of delinquency, they are less often described in terms of moral character traits, and they commonly manifest more social conformity than boys. Few sex differences have been reported from the many studies of guilt and of resistance to temptation. However, boys appear to be more oriented to general notions of the application of rules and of justice, and to be less inclined to blame or coerce others for the same faults as they themselves possess, an indication of more 'moral' behaviour on the part of boys. These, however, are only some instances of the characteristics of the sexes, and more detailed accounts are available elsewhere (e.g. Kohlberg, 1963); but they clearly raise important issues for teachers and those concerned with the curriculum.

Social-class differences. Social class, like sex and age, has been an important basis for the investigation of moral characteristics, much of the interest having been stimulated by the tendencies noted already for parental rearing practices to differ across socio-economic groups. Among other things, comparisons between groups of working-class and middle-class children have shown that working-class children reveal less guilt, express more direct aggression in story-telling situations and tend to behave more aggressively in school; that various measures of conscience are related to social status; and that middle-class children tend to make more mature moral judgements and are less likely to express preference for immediate tangible rewards.

However, social-class comparisons are beset with difficulties, for class reflects not only differences within families from various backgrounds, for example, in the use of reasoning, extent of verbalization and social conventions, but also in neighbourhood conditions and values, peer contacts, and type and quality of education. Since teachers find themselves working within this gross complex, then comparative findings can be informative at the descriptive level; but the involved nature of social-class influences makes it difficult to proceed beyond descriptive labelling of children to explanations of differences in moral characteristics. Indeed, through the failure in some studies to take account of the many complications, misleading explanations have arisen, for example, in attributing different characteristics to social-class groups which largely disappear when a factor such as IQ is taken into the reckoning.

Interaction in small groups

Encounters with members of the family, and especially with its mother, are dominant in the first three years of a child's life. This is a period when he is acquiring the language, motor skills and conceptions of the environment without which subsequent interaction with other adults and with those of his own age would be grossly restricted. By four or five years he is managing co-existence and has widened affectional ties to include many others beyond the family, and by seven he is usually established in the structure of a stable peer group, able to manage for himself his affairs with other children, responsive to their views and bound to them by affection and influence.

Children's groups arise from propinquity. Opportunities to encounter others tend to produce further encounters; and liking expressed by one child for another tends to produce reciprocated liking. In addition, the bringing together of children for formal purposes – to give them nursery-school facilities or to give them instruction through school – creates peer contacts which lead in turn to informal groupings.

Whether the group consists of young pupils in a classroom, a number of children who share a common interest or a neighbourhood gang of adolescents, it has common features. It will have considerable stability over time, members will tend to interact more with one another than they do with non-members, norms of conduct towards one another and towards outsiders are established, power and affection is distributed among members, and the members will often establish physical territory for their activities to the exclusion of others.

Group membership is usually highly prized, and since children spend a great deal of their time with other members and tend to share similar values and to behave alike, the peer group and the vaguer peer 'culture' exercise the minds of parents and educationists as well as attract the attention of the advertiser and the providers of mass entertainment. It is not surprising then that a great deal of effort has been expended upon their study.

When children are brought together in a classroom, the formal structure is quickly underpinned by the appearance of informal relationships. The developments can be observed; however, the structure of relationships has been most extensively studied through the use of sociometric questionnaires. These indicate that the distribution of affection is unequal, departing in a fairly consistent way from what should be expected by chance. Using the data from an early sociometric study of groups of girls, Zajonc (1966) shows that the number of reciprocating pairs (pupils choosing each other as close companions) is more than twice the chance expectation, that there is a smaller than chance number of unreciprocated choices and that the number of girls who are not chosen at all is considerably greater than chance. The presence of a hierarchy can also be demonstrated in a crude form by summing all the choices given to each group member by the others, in which case a few receive a large number of choices and some none at all, with others stringing out between them. Furthermore, given groups of some thirty pupils, there is considerable structural similarity over them: for those analysed by Zajonc, there were about five isolated girls, thirteen reciprocating pairs and fifty one-way choices per group.

The general impression of a hierarchy conceals a more involved substructure. Thus, in the usual classroom the informal group will have, in addition to its 'star' choice, pairs and isolates, three or four subgroups of four or five reciprocating members, and chains of pupils, connected mutually in a line of pairs. Choices within subgroups largely account for an individual's affectional rating; however, for a high position in the whole group it is necessary to attract choices from two other sources: members of other subgroups or children not attached to subgroups. In both cases these outside choices are usually unreciprocated.

In some groups the substructures themselves are extensively interconnected to give a cohesive whole. Lack of cohesiveness, however, is often apparent where the initial grouping was formally imposed; it can arise from hostility among the preferred pupils of the different subgroups, from accidents of bringing together children who are already informally grouped outside the school, from amalgamating pupils who were previously in different classes and from socio-economic, sexual and ethnic differences. Other sources of low cohesion are found in the lack of perhaps two or three individuals who are widely attractive and in a high degree of self-sufficient pairs.

Social power is also unequally distributed, although not necessarily in the same individual ordering as for attractiveness. Often, of course, the two facets of sociometric status are combined, but there are many ways in which influence may be exerted over others, and various reasons why an individual may seek out someone as a source of advice, information or even protection. Thus, some can have power without being particularly attractive, and a classroom group may have different 'leaders' for relatively specific functions. Where their functions are different within a group, 'leaders' need not be a source of conflict nor of lack of cohesiveness, but where they are the dominant individuals of subgroups with distinctive values, rather than pupils with specific qualities which are admired across the whole group, they can be disruptive, adversely affecting the group itself and the management by the teacher of the formal class.

Many attempts have been made to generalize about the bases for attraction and power. Investigators have studied a wide range of social antecedents and personal attributes – social class, birth order, intelligence, personal appearance, and so forth – and have come up with a number of low but often significant associations with sociometric status.

Two social-class tendencies have been reported: for children to be chosen more often by other children of their own social class, and for them to make out-of-class choices of pupils in a higher social class than their own. Among the personal attributes examined, high measured intelligence, physical attractiveness, achievement and physical maturity all correlate positively with acceptance. Children who are high on creativity, aggression, withdrawal or anxiety tend to be low on acceptance. Where children themselves are asked to explain their choices they value friendliness, kindness, honesty, loyalty, even temper, tidiness and good looks.

Social antecedents and personal traits are some guide to power and attraction among children, but have limited predictive value. In typical situations they do little to explain why one child should be preferred over another or why particular friendships are formed. A major limitation lies in the kind of trait descriptions used to delineate the popular and the unpopular. They represent little more than crude impressions of what individuals are like or should be like. More precise behavioural descriptions of the techniques which children use in their encounters might be more enlightening. Secondly, the trait approach has a ring about it of fixed qualities for success or failure in group relations, neglecting the composition of the group and the availability to pupils of various techniques for meeting the demands imposed by the particular circumstances in which they find themselves.

Merei's (1949) experiments with nursery groups showed how the particular group context can modify children's performance. Noting which children were dominating or lacking in influence, he gathered the less effective ones into groups on their own, then later introduced one of the formerly dominant individuals into each group. To begin with, the less effective children soon developed their own groups; group rules of conduct were established and individuals took over specific positions and functions. Out of what had apparently been inadequate resources in the original situation, the ineffective created their own structures of relationships. Then, when the dominant child was introduced he once again became influential, but now alongside the group's own dominant children, and only after conforming to the group rules. This shows the limitations of thinking about performance as the outcome of more or less fixed attributes of individuals; it also demonstrates the collective strength of small groups and the pressures they can exert on those who belong to them or who may wish to participate. Adherence to norms of conduct and of values of groups is a requirement of acceptance; readiness to do so has been demonstrated repeatedly in studies of conformity (e.g. Asch, 1946). The consequences of deviation can also be readily shown – in changing patterns of communication with deviates and, where deviation persists, in communication dropping off rapidly to create effective exclusion.

So far the performance of an individual has been explained in terms of personal attributes, the personal resources of the members of a particular group, and conformity processes. However, it is also dependent upon subtle circularity effects which occur in the course of relationships. Thus, if a child fails to attract others or to establish influence fairly early in the sequence, perhaps because he is in a very attractive league or has difficulty in acquiring the appropriate behaviour, he may lose self-esteem and, in turn, make fewer and less competent attempts to gain recognition. In consequence he may remain low in the hierarchies or will seek acceptance elsewhere. The converse case also applies. That such effects do operate is indicated indirectly by considerable individual stability of status over time and over different groups, and by evidence that leading persons who think that they are more popular than they really are can modify their behaviour.

Interaction and person perception

Over the years children acquire repertoires of social techniques. However, social interaction requires more than the ability to behave in this way or that; it is necessary to know how to behave – or at least to set rough limits – and to be able to make adjustments to behaviour during encounters with others. In order to investigate matters of choice of behaviour it is useful to infer perceptual–cognitive processes intervening between observable acts – processes involving the selection of incoming information, the analysis and evaluation of this information, and decisions as to subsequent acts. The study of these processes has commonly been labelled 'person perception'. It is a difficult and diffuse area of psychology, but deals with such readily familiar topics as the formation of impressions of personality, stereotyping, social sensitivity and self-impressions.

The impressions that individuals form about the personalities of those whom they meet or hear about can result in very distinctive ways of behaving towards them. Kelley (1950) found that when students were provided with brief written descriptions of a guest lecturer, descriptions that were identical except that some were given the impression that he was a 'rather warm' person and others that he was 'rather cold', the warm-cold description subsequently affected the amount of interaction they had with him. Thus, although all the students sat together to hear his lecture, a greater proportion of those who had initially had him described to them as 'warm' participated afterwards in the class discussion. Associations between impressions of others and non-verbal behaviour have now been extensively investigated (see Argyle, 1969, pp. 95–8, 140–43). Physical proximity, relative body orientation, head position, direction of gaze and body posture are all in various ways indicative of perceptions of 'friendliness' and of liking and disliking. Furthermore it appears that such non-verbal behaviour may be relatively more important than verbal behaviour. Unfortunately, no studies have yet been done on teacher–pupil interaction in this context. Other, more familiar, illustrations can be found in stereotypical impressions of ethnic and other groupings, where interaction may be avoided or take discriminatory forms.

With the major exception of 'racial' and national stereotyping there is little evidence upon the early development of person perception. Thus, while adults display major tendencies towards (a) simplifying, classifying and labelling features of their social environment, and (b) going beyond the information available to them on the assumed characteristics of others, it is far from clear how particular patterns of labelling or of trait inferences have been acquired. However, the child's social environment is no less complex than the adult's; indeed, since it is continually expanding and is less predictable than that of the adult there are strong reasons for supposing that personal 'theories of personality' and a wide range of social stereotypes appear early and that considerable modifications take place with age.

Although it tells us nothing about the origins of stereotypes, the work reported by Hudson (1967) is currently of interest in that it deals with the presence of beliefs about the personal characteristics of arts specialists and scientists among able schoolboys. Thirteen- to seventeen-year-old boys, potential arts and science specialists, were asked to rate a number of typical figures (for example, novelist, physicist, mathematician) on pairs of adjectives. The stereotypical physical scientist emerged as distinct from typical figures in the arts; compared, for example, with the novelist, the physicist was perceived as more dependable and hard working, less imaginative and less warm and exciting. Ratings of typical wives differed also, the novelist's wife being more exciting, feminine, soft and imaginative. These results were substantially the same for boys of all specialisms, and as pronounced for thirteen year olds as for the specialists of seventeen. As Hudson points out, popular preconceptions about the personal lives of scientists may help to explain the problems of recruitment to the physical sciences. If this is so then it would be of great practical interest to search further back among primary schoolchildren for the origins of these stereotypes.

Since children spend a great deal of their time with one another it seems likely that implicit 'theories' about the personal traits of friends and associates would be well established by early adolescence. These 'theories' should be reflected in clusterings of correlated personality traits obtained by asking children to make ratings of one another on lists of personal qualities (for example, courtesy, loyalty, cooperation). An analysis of the peer ratings made by girls in a Scottish secondary school (Morrison and Hallworth, 1966) indicated three main 'dimensions' on which peers were perceived and assessed. Furthermore, the results suggested that the perceptions of adolescents are modified considerably both by the age of the raters and by the sex of those rated. The thirteen-year-old raters had co-operation with teachers, sociability and interests respectively as the key items in defining the three 'dimensions'; but for the fifteen year olds, other traits, generosity, gentleness and maturity, were salient. When they were rating boys, the younger girls gave particular attention to the confidence, appearance and interests of a boy, but the older girls emphasized his maturity, strength, stability and leadership. Also, each age group had its own view on prefect suitability; the younger girls, when rating either sex, associated it with the 'pleasant classmate', that is, with the traits of courtesy, generosity, loyalty and co-operation with teachers, whilst for the older girls, the boy who was suitable as a prefect was the 'non-academic leader', as defined by leadership, games ability, maturity and strength.

One aspect of person perception still to be considered concerns the need to perceive and comprehend the motives and feelings of others as well as their personal traits. Social sensitivity, that is, the ability to perceive and comprehend more or less accurately motives and feelings, is probably an important factor in the development of conceptions of oneself, in the acquisition of behaviours and in shaping the course of interpersonal behaviour. To investigate factors influencing social sensitivity and to examine its associations with children's self-concepts and interpersonal competence, Rothenberg (1968) got elementary-school pupils to listen to tape-recorded conversations which contained expressions of the four common emotions of happiness, sadness, anger, and distress or anxiety. The children were then asked to describe how the actors felt and why they felt in the way they did. Social sensitivity, as assessed from the children's answers to these questions, significantly increased with age (nine and twelve years olds were tested) and with intelligence, but there were no significant associations with the sex of pupils, socio-economic background, family size or position in the family. Pupils rated high by their peers and by their teachers on aspects of interpersonal relations tended to be more socially sensitive, whilst those rated by teachers as low on interpersonal adjustment did particularly poorly in interpreting the stressful tape recordings. Also, there was evidence from the younger children that the more socially sensitive had more favourable conceptions of themselves.

These results do not agree entirely with those obtained by other workers, but there is agreement over the association between social sensitivity and competence in personal relations. This being so, it would be valuable to know how, if at all, this skill (or more likely, complex of skills) might be fostered. At present, such information is lacking.

Perceptions of others influence interpersonal behaviour, but what, if any, are the effects of an individual's perception of himself? Does one's self-esteem, that is, the extent to which a child or adult believes himself to be capable, successful and worthy, affect behaviour and the assessments others make of a person? There is a widely held belief that it does, supported by numerous clinical observations that adults who seek psychological help frequently reveal and acknowledge feelings of inadequacy and unworthiness, and that individuals with doubts about their worthiness find difficulty in establishing close relationships with others and, in consequence, feel and become socially isolated. Furthermore, experimental studies indicate that desire to maintain favourable self-evaluations is a complex interactive factor in striving for social status and approval, and that the possession of a favourable self-perception is associated with resistance to conformity pressures, with high social activity and with effective expression of personal views.

Realistically high self-esteem would appear to be worth having, which in turn leads one to ask how it is acquired, how it correlates with aspects of a child's behaviour and what consequences it has. These three topics have been investigated by Coopersmith (1967) in a major study of pre-adolescents. He argues that 'persons with high, medium and low self-esteem live in markedly different worlds'. Among his children, those with high self-esteem had more friends, said they found it easier to make friends and were more likely to take a directive part in group conversations, whilst those who were low in self-evaluation were more conformist, tended to be listeners, would rather say nothing than risk saying something that might annoy others, were more sensitive to criticism and were more self-conscious. Also, those high on self-esteem had higher academic achievements and were perceived by others as being more academically as well as socially successful.

One particular merit of this study is that it does look at the origins of self-evaluation. Most of the evidence bears upon parental behaviour and relations with children – although some of the findings could also concern teachers. Within the family setting, good relations between parents, family cohesiveness, concern with the child's problems, the appreciation of its achievements, encouragement to the child to express its point of view, and firm, consistent influence upon its behaviour were all associated with high self-esteem.

Education, interaction and influence

The impact of education

The power of educational institutions and of teachers seems so obvious as to be hardly worthy of discussion; it is demonstrated daily in the lasting friendships of former pupils, in the changing social habits of communities, or perhaps most dramatically in the way in which a few teachers manage successfully to organize the activities of several hundred pupils. However, it is far less obvious how they manage to have so much power or how the social performance of pupils – their social techniques, role behaviours and structures of friendship and influence – relates to particular educational policies. It is probably true that the teacher will have a far hazier notion of the sources of his power to control a class than he will have of his teaching subject or methods of instructional techniques. His training will have given a great deal of help with the latter, but rather less on how to increase his social effectiveness with pupils, on how to apply specific social techniques to this or that objective, or on the dynamics of the groups he will work with. In scholastic areas he will be a rational expert; in social ones quite commonly a follower of inherited maxims or of trial-and-error practice.

However, limited knowledge is equally disturbing when it is shown by educationists and others who advocate major educational policy changes on the grounds that they will lead to significant alterations in the social skills, values and interactions of the mass of pupils and subsequently of adults. Such changes, concerned, for example, with school organization or selection procedures, may be introduced with only shreds of evidence, especially on long-term effects, to support them, and in ignorance of facts about social processes which suggest that there are powerful constraints upon the effectiveness of adult-initiated changes.

The social power of the teacher

The ability of a teacher to regulate the social performance of his pupils stems from three sources: (a) the reinforcers at his disposal – praise, attention, physical proximity, resources desired by pupils, (b) the manner in which he distributes his social power and (c) the content of his teaching and the provision he makes for extra-curricular activities. Social reinforcement and distribution of power are particularly important for the immediate and short-term behaviour of pupils, since the skill with which they are handled affects the general climate of the classroom, and the cooperation and learning of the individual. They set the conditions for effective instruction. They can also have more long-term influences on pupils out of school and in later life; however, more is expected in these ways from the curriculum and extra-curricular activities – instruction on sex and sexual behaviour, experience of social–occupational role behaviour, participation in groups doing field studies. Whilst a great deal is now known about short-term effects of teachers, this is not so for the more far-reaching outcomes, partly because longitudinal studies in schools have been lacking and partly because of the great technical difficulties in doing follow-up studies into adult life.

Most of the work on teachers' uses of social reinforcers is of recent origin. The delay has been due to the need for thorough classroom observation techniques, and to the traditional use of survey rather than experiment in research on teachers. However, impressive evidence is now available to show that teachers can readily be trained to change specific aspects of their behaviour towards pupils and that apparently small modifications can have dramatic effects. An excellent illustration is given by Madsen's investigation (Madsen, Becker and Thomas, 1968) of two teachers of elementary-school classes; he got them to vary systematically their use of 'giving rules', 'praising appropriate behaviours' and 'ignoring inappropriate behaviours'. During the experimental conditions, observers recorded the behaviour of three target pupils – pupils whose behaviour was particularly troublesome – and reported impressions of the total classroom climate. In the one class, teacher A generally maintained control through scolding and loud critical comments: 'there were frequent periods of chaos, which she handled by various threats'. Her most difficult pupil was Cliff: 'he did not respond to the teacher's questions ... scratched himself repeatedly, played in his desk, paid no attention to assignments ... continually made blowing noises ... and would leave the room without permission'. The observers noted that he tried to talk to other children who in turn ignored him, and that he was concerned with the little girl behind him, for whom he had a sign on his desk which read, 'Do you love me?'. During the experiment he showed little change until teacher A started praising appropriate behaviour – in fact, he got worse during the 'ignore inappropriate behaviour' phase. To begin with it was very difficult for the teacher to find anything to praise, but as praise continued he began to work harder at assignments, learned to ignore other children who were misbehaving, started to seek the teacher's attention and eventually moved up to the top arithmetic group.

Madsen concluded that giving rules alone exerted little effect on classes, but that ignoring poor behaviour and praising appropriate actions was highly effective, with praise being the key to effective management. Furthermore, the study demonstrated that praise as a reinforcer not only affected the target pupil but improved the whole class–teacher relationship, one reason being that the effective reduction of the misbehaviour of one child meant less 'ripple' effect across the group.

Reinforcement applied to a few specific aspects of a child's behaviour has general repercussions. This collateral social development has also been demonstrated by Buell, Stoddard, Harris and Baer (1968); a pre-school child who was poor in motor and social development was socially reinforced by teachers to use outdoor play equipment. Use of play equipment increased and the tactic then led to more social interaction with other children and a marked decrease in some baby-like behaviour.

These examples concern young children and there does not appear to be comparable evidence on the reduction of troublesome conduct among adolescents. Since older pupils may have more deeply ingrained patterns of conduct, they may be much more resistant to the effects of single, specific reinforcers like praise – either they would be unresponsive or, as seems more likely, would require longer treatment, which, in turn, puts greater strain upon teachers, especially over ignoring inappropriate behaviour.

Observation and personal experiences indicate that teachers differ considerably in the extent to which they disperse their power in the classroom. Some hold a tight personal control over events, concentrating management and decisions in their own hands, while others delegate responsibilities to pupils, give them a greater say in significant decisions and place more reliance upon the social power of the pupils themselves to regulate group behaviour. Furthermore, the extent to which devolution of power is practised often relates to the degree of emotional responsiveness and concern for pupils' feelings shown by the teacher. Variations in these two broad aspects of teachers and of schools are reflected in such popular labels as 'traditional–modern' or 'authoritarian–democratic'. Whilst the labels serve as little more than irritants, the distinctions being attempted are important. Many investigations have now been done (see Hoffman and Hoffman, 1966) which show that dispersion of power and emotional acceptance are associated with: (a) more pleasant social–emotional climate in the classroom, less conflict and anxiety among pupils, and increased self- and mutual esteem among them, and (b) more frequent pupil interaction, wider dispersion of social power within the peer group, and more self-initiated work and personal responsibility for actions.

These are all immediately observable effects within a class or an entire school. However, they are so pervasive that it is likely that some at least persist in long-term characteristics of pupils – this is certainly the impression of some secondary-school teachers about the pupils who come to them from primary schools where 'modern' methods are practised. More lasting effects beyond school are generally unknown.

The effects of the curriculum are undoubtedly the most difficult to establish, for although it has implicit social objectives, its impact is highly sensitive to over-riding influences of the home and the peer group, to the differing possibilities for social education in the various subject areas and to the teacher's treatment of material, and effectiveness in class management.

Schools bring teachers and pupils together, concentrated for scholastic functions which cannot readily operate elsewhere. The academic authority of teachers stands out. However, propinquity is double-edged; it gives teachers exceptional facilities for controlling the young and for imparting information and opinions, but also creates informal peer structures in classroom and school. These informal groups have their own codes and forms of conduct, which may or may not be agreeable to teachers, and can exert greater influence over their members. Berenda (1940), for example, found that elementary-school pupils, who were making judgements in situations where judgements had also been made by either peer or teacher confederates of the experimenter, were more likely to accede to peers and to say of the teacher that perhaps she couldn't see properly! Teachers, in fact, are less likely to be social than academic authorities, especially where they are perceived by pupils as socially inexperienced, show embarrassment in handling important social concerns of pupils or give little more than social prohibitions. Schofield (1968), writing on sexual behaviour, quoted some pupils' views on their teachers:

'It was all rather vague. I thought it embarrassed him as much as it embarrassed us' (boy, aged 15).
'We had the lot – even the sex life of the broad bean' (girl, aged 16).
'Before we left, the Reverend told us not to do it, the doctor told us how not to do it and the head told us where not to do it' (boy, aged 18).

In the same survey, the peer influences upon patterns of sex information and upon sexual behaviour were highlighted. By far the largest number of subjects learnt the 'facts of life' from their friends at school, and the sexually active 'tended to find out about sex from their friends and to eschew information or advice from their parents'. The sexually experienced girl was more likely to be in a mixed group and the experienced boy to spend a great deal of time with his group. Schofield also found that non-experienced boys tended to think of their friends as having more sex than they did and suggests that 'this, combined with the strong pressures towards conformity in teenage groups, must be one of the influences that leads a boy on to sexual experimentation'.

Wherever schools are publicly financed and controlled, the social influence which teachers try to exert is likely to be towards the codes of morality which are publicly endorsed by high-status sections of the society, towards an 'official' morality. In this they may or may not be supported by pupils' parents or by their peer groups. Thus the influence of middle-class parents is more likely to be in the same direction as that of teachers than is that of working-class parents; and the influence of the peer group will be counter to that of teachers in so far as its values involve a commitment to the 'teenager' role. Sugarman (1967), for example, found that ratings of pupils' conduct made by their teachers were related to both these factors.

An assumption which must be challenged, however, is that teachers and at least middle-class parents generally attempt to influence adolescents towards the same moral standards, as must the assumption that peer-group influence is almost inevitably opposed to that of teachers. Studies of individual schools (e.g. Hargreaves, 1967) show cases of pupil groups exerting strong pressures on peers to accept 'official' values; and other evidence that pupils from all social classes found much greater satisfaction of their expressive needs at home than at school, especially with regard to freedom and self-direction, suggested that the moral values upheld by teachers may be less acceptable to adolescents than those upheld by their parents. An interesting study by Paton and Beloff (1970) raised these questions in an international context. With a sample of predominantly middle-class Scottish twelve year olds, they replicated an experiment earlier carried out in Moscow and in New York. The children were asked to say how they would react in a number of situations involving moral dilemmas, to each of which, according to the 'official' moralities of all three countries, one of the responses was clearly correct. After responding in the 'neutral' situation, the children were asked to give two other sets of responses, one in the belief that their parents would see their answers, the second in the belief that their answers would be seen by their peers. Soviet children were much more 'moral' than American and Scottish children; but, more significantly, they responded in the direction of increased morality under both parent and peer 'pressure'. American children, on the other hand, responded with greater morality under parent pressure, but with less morality under peer pressure. Among the Scottish children, peer pressure had a similar but greater effect than it had on the Americans, but parent pressure had an insignificant effect. These results both demonstrate the effectiveness of the deliberate use which Soviet teachers make of peer pressure and also suggest that British teachers may tend to be at the opposite extreme, attempting to train pupils in moral standards which are not actively supported by either parents or peers.

Although academic and occupational objectives are overriding in the treatment of most conventional school subjects, most curricula are, with varying degrees of explicitness, intended to influence pupils' social skills and values. Both the subject content and the methods by which it is taught may contribute to the achievement of such goals. Thus one would expect that regular participation in co-operative projects would have different effects upon interpersonal behaviour from those of being lectured or of working individually. History, geography and science subjects may indirectly influence social values; English, especially where it has large oral and dramatic components, may be more directly effective, as can modern studies, where pupils can be aroused to serious discussion of social issues and to civic participation, both of which may directly carry over into post-school behaviour. But in all these cases the variety and diffuseness of the social education given creates many difficulties in objectively assessing general effects upon children.

Possible effects are more susceptible to examination where a subject has primary and explicit goals to influence social behaviour and to help towards interpersonal adjustment now and in the long term. Sex education and religious education are perhaps the two most obvious of such subject areas. Even in these areas, however, the best available evidence is from surveys which have revealed simple statistical relationships without being able to isolate the influence of curricular factors from others or to distinguish among different aspects of the curriculum. Schofield (1968) found that whilst the great majority of girls had received some sex education at school, only half of the boys had; this education was usually in the form of biological and physiological information and only rarely involved description of human sexual intercourse. Those who had received some form of sex education were neither more nor less experienced in sexual activities than those who had not, and from the various sources of evidence Schofield concluded that 'sex education seems to have had remarkably little effect on the subsequent sex behaviour of the teenagers'.

In a large-scale survey of religious education in English county secondary schools, Alves (1968), like previous investigators, found that 'improvement of moral responsibility' and 'insight into moral questions' were among the aims most widely endorsed by teachers of the subject, while over half of them indicated that they also aimed to promote 'personal Christian dedication' among their pupils. One general finding was that sixth-form pupils tended to know less about religion, to be less positive in their attitudes towards Christianity and to attend church less frequently than pupils in fourth and fifth forms. More discriminating than any school variables were regional and sex factors, girls tending to have higher attainment and attitude scores than boys, and '(generally speaking) the nearer one gets to London the less favourable the attitudes towards Christianity become'. Alves used a global criterion measure, in which equal weight was given to attainment and attitude scores, as a basis for selecting schools which were most and least successful. Among the variables studied which differentiated between these two groups were the teachers' experience in RE, the number of extra-curricular societies in the school, the presence of a Christian society among these and the involvement of the school in social service schemes which the RE department has been active in promoting. Teaching methods were significantly related to attitude scores in the London area, with 'reading of textbook with set exercises' appearing to be the most successful method and 'problem-centred discussion' one of the least successful. Commitment to Christianity among pupils was positively associated with authoritarianism and negatively associated with permissiveness. These statistical results, which do not take account of many potentially relevant factors, are best seen as describing an existing situation and giving only tentative indications of possible causative relationships; on the whole, however, one is left with the impression that, even in terms of pupils' verbal expressions of their attitudes, RE teaching is not currently very successful in achieving its social goals.

One of the major difficulties in investigating the effectiveness with which curricula achieve their social goals is that the goals are rarely stated in precise behavioural terms, or even made explicit. One aid to greater precision in the discussion of such non-cognitive objectives is the taxonomy of affective objectives developed by a group of American educationists (Krathwohl, Bloom and Masia, 1964). On a continuum of increasing internalization – the degree to which the ideas or practices of others are adopted as one's own – they distinguished thirteen types of affective objectives, in five main categories:

1. Receiving – willingness to attend to phenomena or stimuli.

2. Responding – willingness to respond to a phenomenon or to engage in an activity and to gain satisfaction from it.

3. Valuing – stable and consistent behaviour that is motivated not by the desire to comply or obey, but by the individual's commitment to an underlying value.

4. Organization – conceptualization of values and their organization into an internally consistent system.

5. Characterization by a value or value complex – habitual behaviour in accordance with a total value system, a 'philosophy of life'.

An important facet of this hierarchical system for

classifying objectives is the relation between the different levels of internalization and different kinds of cognitive activity. Where a teacher's objectives fall within the receiving and responding categories, the only cognitive achievements generally necessary will be for pupils to be adequately informed about the phenomena to which they are to attend or respond; at the higher levels, analytic and synthetic thinking will generally be required.

In so far as current statements of curricular objectives with regard to social education are sufficiently precise to be classified in terms of this taxonomy, many objectives appear to fall within the first two categories. This is so wherever specific types of behaviour are prescribed and where it is the behaviour, rather than the motivation or reason for it, with which one is concerned; the teacher's task is somehow to persuade pupils to behave in a given way. Relevant to such objectives is the extensive body of psychological research on persuasion (see, for example, Rosnow and Robinson, 1967), the results of which suggest, for example, that a communication is likely to be more persuasive if arguments for the favoured course of action are put first and those against it later, and if conclusions and directions for action are made explicit; that, in the long term, the prestige or credibility of the communicator may not affect the extent of opinion change; and that behaviour is more likely to change if individuals can be induced to commit themselves publicly to such change. As yet, however, it is difficult to apply the results of this research with any confidence to teaching in schools. For one thing, persuasive techniques vary considerably in their effectiveness according to the characteristics of those one is trying to persuade. Secondly, there are few simple generalizations which can be derived from research results. For example, is it effective to induce fear in people in attempting to discourage them from smoking? The answer depends on the people and the context, and while some degree of fear may often be useful, if the fear goes above a certain level it will generally lead to negative results.

Finally, very little direct evidence is available about persuasion in the distinctive context of schools, or particularly about its long-term effects.

Many curricular objectives, however, are likely to fall within the higher categories of Krathwohl's taxonomy. Indeed, some teachers have ethical objections to attempts at permanently influencing the social behaviour of pupils in specific and prescribed ways; instead, they would aim to have pupils clarify their own values, choose systems of values for themselves and acquire patterns of behaviour consistent with these values. Taking this type of approach to defining the goals of moral education, Wilson, Williams and Sugarman (1967) suggested that morality can be described in terms of the following components:

1. Accepting other people's feelings and interests as of equal validity to one's own.

2. Awareness of one's own and other people's feelings.

3. Mastery of sufficient factual knowledge to allow one to assess the probable consequences of one's actions.

4. Rational formulation of a set of rules or principles relating to one's own and other people's lives and interests.

5. Ability to translate one's principles into action, to live in accordance with them.

As Wilson and his colleagues admit, both these components themselves and the relations postulated between them need to be defined with much greater precision; but analyses of this nature are a necessary first step if evidence is to become available about the effectiveness of curricula in achieving the social goals to which they are directed, or about how they might be made more effective. At present, there is an almost total lack of such evidence.

Educational organization

Teachers function within schools which form parts of larger educational systems, and formal organization, both within and across schools, affects the deployment of teachers, the distribution of pupils and the degree and nature of social influences. Furthermore, since formal organization can be changed, with changes embracing very large numbers of pupils and teachers, the possibilities for inducing mass social effects appear enormous. It is not surprising, then, that active discussion and fierce debate focus upon it, part of the concern being with key features of internal school organization such as streaming, and part with system characteristics such as selection for secondary education and separation of pupils into distinctive schools, co-education policies and the existence of an independent fee-paying sector. The proponents of non-streaming, of comprehensive versus selective schools, or of co-education rather than single-sex schools, rest part of their case upon the scholastic merits of particular general policies, but equally they press it on broader issues of social–educational values and of the social behaviour of the youth and adult community. Organization, they argue, determines who meets whom; it restricts or encourages social interaction between pupils of different sex, of different socio-economic backgrounds and of various ability levels. Also, it determines who is exposed to what; it affects the degree of exposure to different values, access to varied and extended courses and opportunities for social experiences.

Research is useful in two ways: (a) to determine whether a particular variable has a useful discriminative power, and (b) if it does discriminate effectively, to evaluate the outcomes of different policies. For example, does the placement of pupils in comprehensive rather than in separate academic and non-academic schools mean that the composition of peer groups will be different and, if so, what are these differences? Despite commonly held beliefs, it cannot be taken for granted that there will be differences, since teachers and pupils may be over-riding sources of variation. Also, it is necessary to do more than establish a source and direction of variation; to support major educational policy decisions, findings need to be highly generalizable over the system or an important subsector, and should be of sufficient magnitude to justify major expenditure and reorganization.

However, there are formidable difficulties in doing research at this level. Some stem from arbitrary classifications of schools; for example, it may make little sense to classify a number of schools as 'comprehensive', and then to compare them with other schools, when there are at least four major kinds of comprehensive systems and several types of internal organization. Furthermore, there are so many variations arising from the nature of school catchment areas, community attitudes to schools, the social composition of pupil populations, teachers' attitudes towards types of schools and schools they work in, and novelty effects associated with reorganization, new premises and the like, that crude classification of school type or internal organization can be completely confounded. Also, where attempts are being made to estimate degrees of social influence and to establish patterns of social interaction, measurement can be complicated by needs to construct instruments tapping the less well-defined areas of self-perceptions, social aspirations or 'social adjustment', and, since our interests are often in long-term effects, by having to rely upon retrospective replies from individuals who have left school and on such post-school samples as are readily testable.

It is worth making these points since they help us to look critically at research results and to be wary of jumping to conclusions. Equally, they suggest the danger of relying upon the personal observations and intuitions of individuals who are often 'committed' parties in controversies.

School organization can affect pupils in three major ways within the British state system by deciding whether or not: (a) boys meet and work with girls, (b) those of high, average and low ability and scholastic performance are together and (c) pupils from manual and non-manual home backgrounds are present in the same school. In practice these are not independent factors, so that segregation may mean the preponderance in a school of less able children from

a working-class neighbourhood. Also, non-segregation may
be short of the ideal, as can be the case where a 'comprehensive' school draws upon what is effectively a single-
class neighbourhood. However, when opportunities for interaction are different what happens?

Increased propinquity in non-segregated situations may
be sufficient to ensure that there will be more contact and
interaction across the groupings. According to Pape (1961),
in a study of one comprehensive and one grammar school,
the pupils in the former 'tended to mix socially irrespective of level of ability or form membership, whereas those
in the grammar school . . . are seen to separate themselves
off within the school, both within the classroom and outside, into still finer ability groupings corresponding to the
graded forms'. Also, pupils' friendships may cut across
social classes, although most choices are intraclass and
where they 'go out' they are likely to be towards pupils
from a higher social grouping. This direction of interclass
choices, however, may be less a matter of general class
characteristics than that children tend to find the personal
qualities that are important to them in friendships more
commonly displayed by middle-class pupils (Feinberg,
1953).

Opportunities for contact that exist in non-segregated
situations are not in themselves sufficient to produce radical changes in patterns of social relationships. Although
boys and girls are commonly educated side by side through
primary school and in most secondary schools, friendship
choices are overwhelmingly within single-sex groups between six to seven years and mid-adolescence. Also, since
they are mostly made within small face-to-face groups of
same age peers, and within the framework of the classroom
unit, ability and social-class mixing depend less on the general organization of the school than on the streaming by
ability of pupils and the degree of heterogeneity of the
classroom. In general, then, arguments about the distinctive effects of comprehensive schools hinge upon the internal organization and, in particular, upon whether rigid

ability streaming operates, and upon the extent to which the schools offer additional levels of social organization to that of the class unit as, for example, the provision of school 'houses' containing cross sections of ability, social background and the sexes, and with their own physical accommodation and social activities (see Hind, 1964). The evidence regarding the effects of school organization on patterns of interaction is not impressive, partly, perhaps, because the reported research is small-scale and does not offer a convincing basis for generalization, but far more likely because the factors determining choice have relatively little to do with formal mass organization of pupils.

Research on other aspects of behaviour is restricted and often indirect: some of it suggests considerable and persisting influences from school, some that it has no influence whatsoever. Dale (1968) has carried out studies comparing former pupils from single-sex and co-educational schools, and his subjects (student teachers) reported on their feelings about school and attitudes to the opposite sex. They were asked, for example: 'Did your school life help or hinder you in your relations with the opposite sex?' Forty per cent of men from boys' schools as compared to 5·5 per cent from mixed schools thought that their schooling had been a hindrance – and similarly distinctive results were obtained from girls. Both sexes from the co-educational schools said that they found it easier to work with members of the opposite sex, and co-educated men found it easier to work under the direction of a woman. This is only indirect evidence on actual behaviour and it would be more valuable to have behavioural reports, for example on pre-marital and marital conduct, to establish the full extent of differences and the nature of individual difficulties and lack of skills.

Schofield's survey on sexual behaviour comes nearest to behavioural evidence. His subjects included pupils and former pupils of all the main types of secondary schools. The largest differences in patterns of heterosexual behaviour were between pupils from grammar and secondary-modern schools, boys and girls from the former type tending to be less experienced sexually – a finding that is not explained by school differences in social-class composition since there was no association between class membership and patterns of behaviour. However, no clear differences were established for pupils from day schools versus boarding schools, independent versus all types of state schools or, in the case of girls (but slightly in favour of more experience for boys), for co-educational versus single-sex schools.

School influence may also show itself in the extent of staying on after fifteen. Miller (1961), comparing comprehensive, grammar and secondary-modern schools, found that the comprehensives were more effective in keeping those pupils who would normally have left at fifteen. Egglestone (1965), however, reported that the comprehensive schools had less holding power over the abler pupils than did the selective schools in his survey, and Currie (1962) said that a boys' sample from comprehensive schools showed a 'very strong desire to leave school to be employed and become economically independent of their home ... this was not due to lack of interest or to feelings of resentment of school controls and restrictions'. Decisions as to staying on or leaving school can obviously reflect pupils' satisfaction or dislike of a particular kind of school climate or of a type of school. However, Currie's evidence suggests associations between school organization and pupils' conceptions of their adult roles. In addition to his findings on boys in comprehensive schools, a comparison between pupils in single-sex and co-educational settings indicated that those in the latter exhibited less scholastic motivation. The girls were more oriented to a traditional conception of their role as housewife and mother, whilst the boys were 'interested in being popular with members of the opposite sex and wished to obtain a status symbol, a beautiful girlfriend'. Pupils from the single-sex schools appeared to be more concerned with school success, with staying on at school, and, for the girls, with school progress, appearance and character development.

Differences in personal happiness and satisfaction with school have commonly been reported. Dale found a higher incidence of personal happiness at school among male and female students who had been at co-educational rather than single sex schools, with a strong preference expressed for mixed schools. Average and below average ability pupils in the comprehensives are reported (see Miller, 1961) as having a higher regard for school, the value of its courses and its place in the community than did comparable children in secondary-modern schools, and Currie (1962) suggested that comprehensive schools provide more satisfaction for the bulk of pupils, his evidence consisting of a lower incidence of emotional upsets and tensions associated with learning, greater expressed interest in school subjects and stronger feelings of personal success.

Terms like 'personal happiness' and 'feelings of success' reflect the concern for examining the school's role in shaping pupils' conceptions of themselves. Formal education seems likely to influence greatly the dimensions on which pupils make their judgements and the positive or negative evaluations they hold about themselves, since it leads to a lengthy comparative exposure to prestigeful and popular teachers and peers, and also introduces pupils to criteria for self-judgement which are commonly held in high regard, e.g. scholastic performance. Furthermore, variations in school organization may exert differential effects, segregation or inclusion on grounds of sex, ability and socio-economic status affecting the kind and range of available comparisons of self against others.

Segregation by ability, whether by selection for different types of schools or by streaming within schools, is a highly potent factor. It leads to comparisons on the highly salient dimension of educational and occupational 'success', is known to be associated with teachers' attitudes and behaviour towards pupils and, in the case of streaming, creates peer groups which correspond closely to school 'success' divisions.

Personal accounts and school investigations (Hargreaves,

1967; Pearce, 1958) indicate the depressing effects of stream-ing upon some pupils. Some of the school type studies men-tioned already also support the view that some forms of segregation have comparable effects. On the other hand, Soares and Soares (1969) found that 'disadvantaged' students in their neighbourhood schools had, if anything, more favourable self-concepts than 'advantaged' students from schools in more prosperous middle-class areas. One of the difficulties in interpreting findings is the lack of com-parison between types of assessments made by different studies, but several other factors are likely to confound simple explanations based upon school type. Some forms of segregation, especially of the neighbourhood kind, in-sulate the less able from the harshest comparisons with those from scholastically more favourable backgrounds; educational 'success' may be irrelevant as a basis for self-evaluation for some pupils so that their relative failure in school hardly affects them; and, since their schools may offer prestigeful criteria other than scholastic 'success' for assessing one's worth, pupils can find other sources of posi-tive self-evaluations. It would be valuable to have a great deal more information about pupils' self-concepts. At pre-sent, neither the general nor specific educational influences are clear.

Conclusion

In bringing individuals together in the classroom and school, formal education becomes a potent means of social influence: it enables adults to deploy their social power with great effect as teachers of classes and as con-trollers of encounters between major categories of pupils; and it creates informal peer groups in which processes of social structuring, friendship choice, person perception and conformity can operate with powerful and lasting effects on interpersonal behaviour.

Research has helped greatly to clarify the nature of the processes underlying social learning and interaction. It has provided impressive evidence of the effects of teachers' behaviour upon pupils in school, showing, for example, how the use of social reinforcers and of dispersion of power can dramatically influence the behaviour of classes and individuals. Furthermore, it has demonstrated both the immediate and lasting effects of the peer group upon its members. A great deal of the evidence in these areas is sufficiently precise and generalizable to be of immediate practical value to teachers and to students in training.

Investigations of the long-term influences of teachers and of school organization upon social performance and attitudes have been less rewarding. Far less has been done and there are many design and assessment problems. Two of the persisting difficulties standing in the way of the analysis and description of organizational influences are the lack of a theoretical basis for the exploration of school organization, and the need to apply some conceptual order to a host of disparate 'attitudes', 'aspirations' and 'feelings' used in the study of pupils. Each investigation stands on its own bit of territory, with its own *ad hoc* hypotheses, and uses measures which can only be compared in restricted ways. Long-term influences are undoubtedly present, as shown by some of the work on co-education, but their extent and magnitude for individuals or for major groupings of pupils are imperfectly understood.

3 Politics and Education

This chapter is concerned with the political attitudes of young people and with the ways in which education may affect the development of beliefs, feelings and behaviours.

What are we to understand by political attitudes? In one sense we may be referring to the views of individuals on political parties and on the organization of community life, and to their personal participation in decision making or in the execution of local and national policies. Here, of course, we are dealing with matters which typically concern adults, since children have few opportunities for direct participation. However, politics in this sense forms part of a much broader topic which deals with the development of awareness, orientation and information about the political system. A great deal of evidence has now been accumulated to show that attitudes towards systems and their parts have their origins in childhood. This topic of political socialization forms a major section of this chapter. Until fairly recently, however, the predominant interest in political attitudes was in views held about groups of people other than one's own group – national, racial and religious – and more especially in the formation and modification of negative prejudices, such as those shown towards minority groups of Negroes and Jews in the United States of America. Intergroup attitudes form the second topic of this chapter.

There is widespread educational interest in both topics. It is treated here in two ways. Firstly, on the assumption that it is valuable and interesting to teachers, carrying on their work in schools, to know something of the developmental background to children's political attitudes, the first part of the chapter gives descriptive findings. The second part deals more directly with the possibilities inherent within educational systems, schools and classrooms of influencing the views and actions of pupils and students. Where possible we have drawn upon school-based studies. However, a great deal of the work done on influencing attitudes has consisted of short-term experiments. Some work of this kind has been included because it offers more controlled evidence – although in terms of the subjects and techniques employed it may have limited relevance in the specific situations of the school, and assumes facilities and expertise in instruction which may be difficult to come by.

The acquisition of political values

Political socialization can be seen as the processes by which political systems maintain themselves against breakdown or radical change. The stress here is upon the conservative tasks of transmitting appropriate attitudes from one generation to the next. Various agencies such as the family, the school and the mass media are involved in (a) developing favourable evaluations of the existing system; (b) creating an awareness of belonging to a community and to a country, and of loyalty and obligations towards them; and (c) establishing information on the structure and functions of government.

Studies done in recent years by American political scientists (e.g. Greenstein, 1965; Hyman 1959) show that several elements of system support are present in primary-school children; that they take the form of preferences and allegiances; and that they appear before children possess any body of information or have any coherent grasp of concepts and principles needed for thinking as compared to feeling about political affairs.

Politicians and political roles

The first signs of political awareness among American children focus upon salient personalities. Asked to look at pictures of symbols of government and to indicate which pictures best showed what government is, eight year olds chose most frequently those of Washington and the incumbent President (Hess and Easton, 1960). No one was so well known as the President, for whom the great majority expressed respect, admiration and loyalty. Sigel's (1968) work on children's images of President Kennedy showed that the children were most impressed by his apparent kindness, approachability, courage and warmth, and rather less by characteristics which older people admired such as his energy, intelligence and wit. It seems that their image was not just based upon impressions about Kennedy as a private individual; the children made relatively few references to his role as a family man. Moreover, other work indicates that political roles as well as incumbents are held in high esteem by children. Many children, then, are initially disposed towards benevolent political images; they tend to maintain them into adolescence, but as they do so the basis for evaluations shifts from the area of personal traits to that of political actions. However, these findings are drawn largely from samples of white children in reasonably prosperous areas. They do not necessarily hold for minority and underprivileged groups where there is some evidence that malevolence more appropriately describes early perceptions of politicians (Jaros, Hirsch and Fleron, 1968).

Political cynicism and efficacy

System support is also shown by children's impressions of the individual's say in the affairs of government and of their faith in politicians. Greenstein (1965) found little evidence amongst nine year olds of the cynicism found in many adults. Following this up with senior students in high schools, Kent Jennings and Niemi (1968b) obtained similar results. They comment that 'the students may be retreating from an even more trusting attitude held earlier, but compared to parents they still see little to be cynical about in national political activity'. Cynicism appears to be held in check over a very extended period which is quite remarkable in face of the long period of exposure to the realities of the political scene and to generally more cynical parents and other adults. Political efficacy, as assessed by responses to questions about the influence of individuals upon affairs, appears as a coherent attitude among nine year olds (Easton and Dennis, 1967). Thereafter, increasing age is associated with the spreading of the attitude among children and a marked change towards a greater sense of efficacy. Thus, by fourteen, over half of their age sample could be assessed as 'high' on the measure they used.

System principles

Measures of efficacy and cynicism tap feelings and judgements by getting responses to statements about the behaviour of politicians and governments. Systems support can be examined also at the level of general principles of government. Such principles may be expressed in a written constitution, in which case they can readily be used as statements with which subjects can be asked to agree or disagree. Horton (1963) used the American Bill of Rights as a basis for studying the attitudes of sixteen- to seventeen-year-old high-school students towards freedom of the individual, and found that one in five of the subjects did not agree with 'freedoms' stated in the Bill, the proportions being considerably larger on some specific items. A comparison with survey results obtained from fourteen year olds suggested that with increasing age there was greater certainty about beliefs and greater acceptance of the Bill. The trend reported here towards more favourable evaluations of 'liberal' principles agrees with findings from other sources (e.g. Adelson and O'Neil, 1966; Rutherford, 1966) that children and younger adolescents are relatively authoritarian.

Partisanship

Different political attitudes commonly become institutionalized in political parties and, while a minority of adults are active paid-up members of parties, the majority have more or less stable allegiances, even if these find only occasional expression through voting for one political candidate rather than another. One of the most interesting results to come out of research is that partisan orientations are amongst the earliest signs of political awareness. In his study of New Haven children, Greenstein (1965) found that party identification was common; by the fourth grade nearly two-thirds of the children were able to say whether their preference was Republican or Democrat, a striking figure if one notes that the proportion of adult Americans identified with parties was not much greater, and that the children's preferences correlated appropriately with the demographic patterns of adult partisanship in the community. Furthermore, partisan allegiance probably remains stable for the majority of children, tying in quite closely with parental party preferences. In his study of English adolescents Abramson (1967) found that 85 per cent expressed a party preference and among them 67 per cent of those with Conservative parents said they would vote Conservative and 77 per cent of those with Labour parents said they would rate similarly. However, only one-third of boys with Liberal parents expressed Liberal support.

Party orientations precede knowledge of party differences or stands on particular issues. Only 6 per cent of the New Haven thirteen year olds were able to cite party differences that were in any sense political whilst among the seventeen year olds of another sample there were still only 16 per cent who noted a broad ideological difference between parties and a further 10 per cent who cited differential group benefits. By this age they have nearly reached adult levels of performance. Neither parents nor children have much knowledge to back their allegiances.

The acquisition of political knowledge

In order to think as well as feel about politics children have to make three major advances. Some political information has to be acquired and the bits ordered into reasonably coherent and related stores – information on institutions and their functions, on the policies and actions of persons and countries, on the geography of politics. Secondly, concepts have to be acquired, such as nation, community, government, foreignness and the like, many of which are inseparable from the grasp they have of fundamental ideas about space and time. And thirdly, they have to develop sophisticated modes of thinking which enable them eventually to apply principles, to analyse problems from standpoints other than their own, to form and to test hypotheses, and to use in a selective and analytic fashion the information and concepts they possess. One finds in fact that some individuals manifest much less cognitive skill than others, but these advances are made by most by the age of sixteen or seventeen (Adelson and O'Neil, 1966; Hallam, 1967).

Ideas of community and government

Young children are surrounded by concrete instances of an organized community; they are able to recognize at five or six years of age the services provided for their family and others, are able to say that it is the government that runs the country, and may know the office and name of Prime Minister; but they are far from having the wider and sophisticated grasp of relationships and obligations implied by the ideas of government and community.

Important advances in understanding are made within childhood itself. To begin with, children must modify their personalized view of government. This is difficult. American studies have shown that the personal figure of the President is the first focus on government; he is the one who matters and Congress is viewed as a group that takes orders from him and performs certain tasks at his command (Hess and Easton, 1960). In fact, there is a persisting tendency into adulthood for individuals to be more aware of the activities of executives than of legislators. Greenstein (1965) found that whilst there was steadily increasing information with age, understanding of different levels of government and of the relationship of various elements developed slowly and unevenly. His American subjects were first aware of the institutions and persons of federal and local government, with state government lagging behind; and at each level of government awareness of the executive preceded that of legislature, with the latter frequently perceived as having a subordinate function. English children first think of the Queen as the effective ruler, regarding her and her role with affection and respect, whilst the Prime Minister is seen simply as another individual whose office is not held in any particular awe. Political realism increases, of course, with age, but at twelve years of age the great majority of children of average ability still view the Queen as more important than the Prime Minister in the running of Britain.

Other changes are taking place in children's notions about the community. Jean Piaget (see Piaget and Weill, 1951) was the first to examine the appearance and consolidation of national identity and of belongingness or foreignness. Swiss children were asked questions about Switzerland and its cantons and were also encouraged to make simple drawings. The six year olds were aware of little more than their personal immediate territory. Although they might say that Geneva was in Switzerland the two would be drawn as circles side by side, and they would maintain that one could not be Swiss and Genevese at the same time. From seven to eight years the idea of spatial inclosure was grasped, but the logical inclosure still caused difficulty for them. However, by eleven years of age most had got the idea of the country with its related and included parts. When all the children were questioned about foreigners the youngest had considerable difficulty, foreign being something absolute rather than relative, so that foreigners were people belonging to other countries and the Swiss could not be foreigners even when they were outside their own country. Jahoda (1963) subsequently did a study with Scottish children, using interviews and a performance test. The youngest again had no more than a vague grasp of local territory and in the test typically arranged the pieces in such ways as to suggest that Glasgow was not included in Scotland. Not until eleven could most of the subjects correctly express in verbal form the relationship Glasgow–Scotland–Britain and arrange the pieces of the test in correct order of size and inclusion.

Piaget has pointed to two changes in thinking between six and twelve. Firstly, the child has to make considerable efforts towards 'decentration' – the broadening of centres of interest from the parochial to larger and more abstract entities. Typically, this development towards a clearer concept of 'nation' comes after the appearance of nationalist sentiment. Secondly, egocentricity has to give way to a 'sociocentric' outlook; that is, to develop the ability to see matters from points of view other than his own and to recognize, for example, that what holds for oneself in a particular situation can also hold for others in an equivalent one.

Changes in ways of thinking about civic affairs are described in Adelson and O'Neil's work (1966). They interviewed students between the ages of eleven and eighteen, presenting them with a number of community 'problems' and recording the ways in which the subjects sought to resolve the issues involved. Their material included 'the introduction of a vaccination law', 'a landowner who was stubbornly resisting the takeover of his property for a community project' and 'the provision and extension of public education'. Before the age of thirteen most of the students were unable to get beyond personalized modes of discourse on political matters. They found it hard to imagine the social consequence of political action; government was still conceived in terms of specific and tangible services; and they were unable to grasp the legitimate claims of the community upon the individual. By fifteen a great many changes had or were beginning to take place. Formal thought was applied now to the issues before them; issues were taken up from different points of view and there was a greater use of principles for making political judgements; they were now able to envisage the long-term social consequences of different courses of action and were less likely to opt for authoritarian solutions; and the earlier tendency to treat institutions and social processes upon a model of persons and personal relationships had largely disappeared.

Considerable changes in pupils' conceptions of the law and of those who administer it are also apparent (Shiels, 1970). Through interviews and essays, ten- and fourteen-year-old pupils were asked to give their views about the origins and purposes of the law, the processes of the legal system, and policemen. Age differences were consistently found, but little evidence of social class, sex or IQ variations. The younger children were unable to get away from a personal approach even when an abstraction or social perspective was called for. Understanding of the law was closely tied to self-experience and whilst they might try to reach a more abstract position they constantly fell back on an exemplary mode of response. A small number throughout insisted that the law was a man who went about catching people, and almost half of the group thought that the law was made by the policeman, judge or some other authority figure. The younger group were more inclined to see laws as performing a negative, coercive function – and as having an authority against which they were powerless. On the administrative side more knowledge about the structure of the legal system was found among the older group, although there was generally ignorance of courts and court processes. Only the younger ones saw the policeman, who was considered infallible by most, as there to impose a necessary obedience. The older pupils more often credited the policeman with admirable rather than tough qualities, with a peace-keeping rather than an investigatory role. Over all, then, changes not only reflected more basic information, but also modifications in conceptions of the functions of law in the community, and in perceptions of those who serve its purposes.

Human conflict

Very little work has been done on knowledge of conflict, yet this is a central theme in the study of government and community. What are the child's notions of war? What knowledge does he possess on the sources of conflict? How does he see conflict as affecting himself and others?

One approach to these questions has been that of taking a known pattern of international relations and examining the child's views about it. In a study of Scottish pupils (Morrison, 1967), the context used was that of East–West relations in recent years. At the age of thirteen children made significantly more favourable evaluations of West as compared to East countries (e.g. USA *v*. Russia and China), coupled with highly distinctive views on the kinds of relations that Britain should have with the governments of the two groups. These preferences formed one element in a larger repertoire of knowledge and judgements. Thus, many of the children were sensitive to ideological differences between the communist and non-communist countries and this awareness provided a background against which the appropriateness of various kinds of actions was judged. Also, likely sources of major conflict were recognized, as was the mutual responsibility which these countries would have for any war that should occur.

Clearly the young adolescent can have considerable understanding of a dominant conflict of modern times, but it is of more fundamental interest to examine over the years the development of general ideas about conflict. P. Cooper (1965) has attempted to do this in a series of studies on war and peace, comparing samples from different countries and age groups on their images of war and peace, the morality of war, justifications for going to war and its necessity, and views on war in the future.

Marked changes are again apparent with increasing age. The bulk of associations with the word 'war' made by young English primary-school children concerned weapons of war and to a lesser extent to types of men involved (soldiers and sailors), and these associations were strongly coloured by the portraits of conventional war which had been retailed to them – in this case, the Second World War. With older children and adolescents the earlier associations were gradually replaced by recognition of the actions and consequences of war and by an increase in emotionally unfavourable references to war. Questioned on the roles of Japan and England in the Second World War, there was increasing consensus with age on Japan being in the wrong. With regard to motives, Japan is accused of making an attack based upon national pride, feelings of inferiority or desire to expand, whilst England was morally correct to defend herself. An underlying feature of the various arguments about conventional war was the increasing awareness of human motives in shaping conflict. The eight year olds often argued that war was not necessary, and placed their faith in deterrence, but the adolescents generally accepted that it was necessary, particularly in defence of country and family, because undesirable motives exist in human beings and influence their behaviour. Finally, views on war in the future changed. Up to twelve years of age the children typically thought that there would be a nuclear war within fifteen years, but they put their probability of survival high and also that of their fellow pupils; the older pupils, however, frequently said that war would not occur, but if it did, expressed less likelihood of survival for themselves and virtually nil for their fellows.

Research into the development of political cognitions is difficult to do and, as is the case with some of Cooper's findings, can be hard to interpret. Understanding is sometimes difficult to disentangle from rote information, and the individual's affective involvement in the content of test and interview material can slant responses or lead to ones that under-represent the quality of his thinking. Despite these problems the effort is worthwhile. The greatest gaps in our knowledge are in the political thinking of pupils in the first years of secondary education. There is already sufficient evidence to show that this is a crucial period in the pupil's development. Only by further work will it be possible to tie up evidence with the work that teachers do or might do to foster the growth of understanding and of more rational political thinking.

Personal ideologies

One danger of neglecting the cognitive aspects is that of giving the impression of political development as a largely passive process in which the individual is moulded by external forces to the virtual exclusion of any self-organizing activity. However, this view is highly implausible on a number of grounds. Increasing sophistication of thought arises from the individual's efforts to explore and make sense of the data of the environment in which he lives, and results in personally distinctive ways of selecting, analysing and organizing knowledge about major areas of human activity. Individual and group differences among adults in their ways of organizing political attitudes, and in their bases for judgements, can readily be demonstrated and it is hardly likely that these could have suddenly come into being. And even among children and young adolescents there is some coherence of beliefs and evidence of political judgements being made against some systematic, if simple, set of standards.

The study of personal political ideologies makes it possible to examine not only particular beliefs and evaluations of persons and events but also to identify structures of political judgement which have resulted from the impress of self upon acquired information and evaluation. Recent work by Warr, Schroder and Blackman (1969) on students' judgements of national governments showed that individuals make rather different uses of a considerable range of 'dimensions' for judgement, the most widely used ones being 'autocratic–democratic', 'capitalist–communist' and 'extensiveness of government control'. An earlier study (McIntyre and Morrison, 1967) of the attitudes to international affairs of Scottish and African students in a college of education indicated 'dimensions' of 'Christianity–communism', 'ethnocentrism', 'tradition–modernity of leadership', and 'ideals for progress/practical developments'; and here, the involvement of Africans in their own continent and countries was reflected in a highly distinctive structure of judgements. Judgements are associated also with membership of political groups and, as will be discussed later, with personality characteristics. Thus, in Warr's study, left-wing subjects were more likely to judge governments in terms of 'capitalist–communist' 'distribution of power' and 'social concern', whereas right-wing subjects emphasized 'external influence', and the politically uncommitted stressed 'autocratic–democratic' and 'general competence'.

Intergroup attitudes

Countries and peoples

The first indications of images of countries and peoples take the form of preferences and crude allegiances. Knowledge, even of the most elementary kinds, again trails behind. In one of his studies of nationalism in British children Tajfel (1966) presented the subjects with all six possible pairs of countries formed by America, France, Germany and Russia, and asked them to say which country they liked better in each pair. At six to seven years of age, two-thirds of them agreed upon placing America first or second, and nearly three-quarters on placing Russia third or fourth. Already, consensus was high but, by nine to eleven years of age 85 per cent placed America or France first or second, with Russia and Germany in the last places. With thirteen year olds, Morrison (1967) used a political distance scale on which preferences could be expressed in terms of the kind of cooperation Britain should have with various countries. This technique has the advantage of using statements which correspond broadly with actual levels of cooperation being practised by countries, so that it is possible to check children's responses against the actual state of relations. Mean rankings indicated preferences for the closest form of cooperation with America, then a considerable drop to a more limited and largely commercial relationship with Russia, then down to virtual non-cooperation with China. There seems, then, to be a fairly close correspondence between the children's attitudes and the actual practices of governments.

Feelings about other countries are accompanied by attachment to one's own. Using a photograph-sorting technique, Tajfel has also shown that children like better those whom they assign to their own national category, and that those who are strongest on national preference tend to make more extreme judgements of others, seeing them as either very similar to their own nationals or very different.

Cross-national investigation, employing comparable age samples (e.g. Lambert and Klineberg, 1967) brings out the interplay of age trends and characteristics associated with national–regional contexts. Young children, for whom parents are the primary source of information about other nationalities, characteristically view foreigners as different from themselves. They employ descriptive rather than evaluative distinctions, referring more to physical features, clothes, language and habits; and there is evidence from their views that particular peoples have been used for training in contrasts. Older children increasingly differentiate people on personality characteristics, politics, religion and material possessions; tendencies to view foreigners as different, strange, unfriendly and bad, decline; and sources of information now stressed are broadcasts and general reading with little reference to parents and teachers as informants.

Comparison of national samples suggests common features such as the tendency for the self-national stereotype to differ from the stereotype held by other nationalities, and for Western nations – USA, France and Britain – to be given preference over others. However, they differ nationally on the amount of affection expressed for others, in the salience of national, regional and ethnic themes in self-national descriptions, and in reasons given for defining other people as like or different from themselves.

Intergroup attitudes and prejudice

The trends we have noted arise from the transmission of popular beliefs and feelings, and from the efforts of children to attain fuller self-concepts, processes fostered wittingly or otherwise by parents, schools and the mass media. One outcome is to produce group preferences, with marked negative prejudice directed at some. Such prejudice is commonly characterized by erroneous beliefs, the attribution of undesirable traits and habits supposedly common to members of the group, discriminatory practices, which may or may not be sanctioned against legally, and sometimes general cognitive and perceptual tendencies within the prejudiced individual (Allport, 1954). It is largely directed in its most unsavoury forms against racial and religious minorities, but its manifestations vary and, depending upon the degree to which it reflects personal needs and dissatisfactions and is supported or not by legal sanctions and social norms, there may be marked prejudice in beliefs, feelings and behaviours or considerable inconsistency from one component to another.

Like people's views on the political system of other countries, prejudice against minorities often has its roots in infancy. Ethnic awareness can appear at the nursery-school stage. From then on, as several American studies (Criswell, 1939; Hartley, Rosenbaum and Schwartz, 1948; Horowitz, 1965; Radke, Trager and Davis, 1949) indicate, there are trends with age towards increased frequency with which hypothetical and actual behavioural choices are directed by white children towards other whites or children in the same or similar religious group, towards the description of self or others in racial terms, and towards the differentiation of situations in which members of the minority can be accepted or should be rejected. These developments in the majority group have parallels in minority children who may show awareness slightly earlier and can also show hostility towards their own group and preferences for members of the majority.

The immigration into Britain of people belonging to various ethnic groups has provided the opportunity for various expressions of prejudice. Kawwa, (1968), for example, surveyed the attitudes of eleven- to seventeen-year-old native

British children and found the usual array of unfavourable views about immigrants – their supposed undesirable personal characteristics (they don't live like us, their living habits and food are bad and disgusting, they are dirty or filthy), their undesirable traits (rude, selfish, greedy, untrustworthy, ignorant) and the social and economic threat they present (they take over houses and jobs, people cannot get houses because of them, they are unfair cheap labour). He found no age or sex differences in attitudes, but the London children he studied were more unfavourable towards immigrants than children from Lowestoft in Suffolk, and made few positive statements about them, whether the subjects of their views were Negroes or Cypriots.

Political attitudes and social influence

In some ways the development of political attitudes follows a common pattern; thus, feelings and allegiances precede knowledge, and as age increases so radical changes take place in modes of thinking; but within this pattern many group and individual differences are apparent. Children grow up with different partisan allegiances, with different feelings and information on attitude objects, and with different perceptions of their political roles.

These variations are assumed to arise largely from differential exposure to sources of social influence, in particular, the community, the family and the school. But, how do these various sources of influence operate, what variations in attitudes arise from different patterns of social exposure and how relatively influential are the sources? Answers to these questions can be offered at several levels of sophistication. In the first instance associations can be examined between political attitudes and categorical variables like social class and religious denomination. This can be taken further into such areas as parent–child similarities in attitudes or educational differences. At this level the answers are of a descriptive and normative kind; they pin down interesting variations in attitudes and their associations with sources, but they may throw little light upon the processes at work. More sophisticated answers take the form of explanations of the processes of influence. They are much more difficult to come by since they involve careful testing of hypotheses, isolation of particular elements of influence within the broader categories like social class, and the recognition that particular sets of attitudes can develop as much from indirect and non-political influences upon individuals as from direct exposure or political instruction. As matters stand then, we can expect to find description well in advance of explanation. Numerous theories exist in the field of political learning but few have substantial support.

Social influences

The processes of attitude formation and change

Several processes have been suggested to account for general trends and for individual and group differences; some are widely applicable, whilst others seem most helpful for understanding the attitudes of specific groups or individuals, or for explaining one aspect of formation rather than another.

Identification. Children form affectional attachments to persons who control resources desired by them and who have the power to reward or to punish. The father is typically regarded as the major identification figure, but children and adolescents identify themselves with other adults, with peers and with institutions. Two possible outcomes of identification are the generalization of the child's feelings about some person in his own life to some political object, and the imitation of the other person's ideas without any direct teaching being involved.

Cumulative learning. Attitudes are based upon general acquisition of bits of information through more or less direct instruction within the family and elsewhere. This leads to a build up of political knowledge over the long term. In the early years the process does not lead to much acquisition of actual information, but a residue of awareness and of feelings remains after the direct instruction has been forgotten.

Cognitive development. Children and adolescents are assumed to be intrinsically interested in interpreting the world around them; this results in major advances in their capacities for acquiring and handling concepts, and for sophisticated appraisal and solution of problems. In the early years the child experiences considerable constraints upon his interpretation of politics so that his feelings and crude categorical labels precede knowledge, the use of principle and 'rational' analyses of affairs.

Psychodynamics. Attitudes towards politics are assumed to reflect the personality system of the individual. Particular sets of feelings and cognitions, then, are acquired in as much as they are compatible with other social values, with personal needs to sustain a particular self-image, and with the working out on others of unacceptable impulses. Another dynamic factor is the effect of motivations like aggression on attitudes. Psychodynamic explanations are most popular in the context of the pathology of extremism.

Normative. Individuals acquire the attitudes that are appropriate to their culture, social class and group backgrounds, and the role expectations that others hold for them. They do so for three main reasons: because these are the attitudes to which they are exposed and they are ignorant of others; because conformity with the views of others and compliance with authority is highly rewarding whilst deviance leads to rejection, loss of status and an uncomfortable degree of uncertainty; and because the appropriate attitudes are the ones most useful or perceived as most useful for effective behaviour in the particular context.

Evidence of one kind or another has been produced in support of all these processes; it is strongest for cognitive and normative processes; the cumulative learning model seems to offer rather better explanation than identification (although this issue cannot adequately be resolved until efforts are made to find out what actually happens in families); psychodynamic arguments are the most speculative (e.g. Adorno, Frenkel-Brunswik, Levinson and Sanford, 1950; Christiansen, 1959) but in some ways the most perceptive.

Categorical variables

Adults from different social classes tend to support different political parties and vary in degree of involvement and participation in politics. Social-class differences are commonly found among children too. Upper-class American children, reported on by Greenstein (1965), were earlier in showing issue orientations in distinguishing between political parties, they responded more frequently in political terms to questions about how they would like to see the world changed, they were more likely to cite public figures as their examples, and were more likely to conceive of politics as a legitimate area for exercising autonomous choice. However, there were no clear differences between upper- and lower-class children either on the likelihood of possessing a party identification (although the upper class were better grounded in information) nor on information about government institutions. In Abramson's study of English secondary-school pupils (1967), middle-class pupils scored higher on political efficacy and public-school boys saw themselves as likely to be more politically effective than did those from state schools. Also, comparisons of pupils in various types of English schools (reflecting different IQ and social-class levels) have shown that grasp of the roles of the Queen and the government is least for working-class children and those in non-selective state schools (Greenstein, 1969). Examination of political ideas in terms of social class does not show such clear cut differences. Whilst Jahoda's results from

Scottish children indicated very significant differences between middle- and working-class schools in the grasp of
relationships between various levels of community and in
recognition of some national symbols, such as the national
anthem and the Union Jack, the relatively poor performance of working-class pupils could largely be accounted
for in terms of the class distributions of measured intelligence.

These findings illustrate some of the difficulty encoun-
tered in using social class as a basis for the analysis of
political development, for to say that individuals belong to
one class or another is to describe a complex of related
tendencies concerning their occupations, rearing practices
and experiences, education, attitudes to authority, abilities,
and social beliefs and values. Thus, explanations for differences in political attitudes can be generated from any
number of single or related elements of the structure. Some
of the differences in political attitudes between social
classes may stem fairly directly from exposure to parental
feelings and cognitions and from the child's position in a
social-class hierarchy; others can arise indirectly from the
transmission by parents, or from the social experiences of
the child himself, of perceptions of his position in the class
structure; whilst yet others develop from the interaction of
social class and education in societies, such as England,
where there is a close relationship between social stratification and selective secondary education. For these and
other reasons, then, social class has little explanatory value
in itself.

Sex differences in political attitudes and in acquiescence
to influence have frequently been reported. P. Cooper
(1965) found that girls at all age levels were less likely to
mention fighting, dying and killing; they were less likely to
make moral judgements in favour of one country rather
than another, or to say that war was necessary and justifiable; and, where they did give justifications for war it
was particularly on the grounds of threat to the family.
Also, they clearly participate less in organized games of

fighting and have less interest in the strategies and methods of war. Among American children (Greenstein, 1965) boys were better informed on politics and, over all for the grades 4 to 8 made significantly more responses of a political nature to questions about interesting news stories. In Morrison's study (1967) girls made rather less favourable evaluations of Russia and of governmental relations with Russia, and Roman Catholic girls produced the largest number of 'anti-Christian' responses to the questions which asked the pupils to say what they understood by communism and why it was disliked by some people. Virtually no attention has been given to the study of such sex differences although to do so would probably give some very interesting information on family socialization practices.

Associations between denominational membership and political attitudes have also been neglected although one might expect denomination to be an influential factor, especially at the level of international affairs, since some denominations clearly feel much more strongly than others about threats to their beliefs, and in some cases operate their own educational systems. At thirteen years of age pupils in Scottish Roman Catholic and non-Catholic schools showed major differences in attitudes towards East–West affairs; Roman Catholic pupils made significantly less favourable evaluations of communism, Russia and China, they generally advocated less close governmental relations between Britain and the two communist powers, and they were particularly sensitized to 'religious' objections to communism. Within a denominational situation, political attitudes are also likely to be influenced by strength of religious feelings so that judgements of other people, countries and policies may fall on the same dimension of evaluation as religion. This appears to be the case in a study of women student teachers in a Scottish college of education where two major dimensions of evaluation were obtained from their ratings of aspects of East–West and African affairs, one of them defined at the one pole by a rating of Christianity and at the other pole by ratings of non-Western countries, politicians and political systems. Here then, a high evaluation of Christianity was associated with low evaluations of other attitude objects which were not directly associated with Christianity or the West.

The evidence on categorical variables like social class and religious denomination, together with the complexity of influence that they imply, suggests firstly that it would be a waste of time to attempt to isolate some specific source of influence to account for the formation of the spectrum of an individual's political attitudes and, secondly, that political attitudes form part of a more generalized outlook upon the environment – to the extent, perhaps, that one is dealing with basic differences in the ways individuals think.

The transmission of parental attitudes

The early appearance of some aspects of political attitudes has focused attention on the family as the first and major source of children's politics. The argument has been bolstered by evidence from parent–child correlations and by the apparent endurance of political attachments from childhood through to adulthood. However, the case for parental influence is not as strong as it is sometimes purported to be. Kent Jennings and Niemi (1968 a and b), for example, have shown that there is a relatively close correspondence between the party loyalties of parents and children; but on issues such as school integration, the holding of public office by communists and freedom to speak out publicly against religion, adolescents diverge from their parents. As a further instance, they cite political cynicism which does not appear to be transmitted. Even when the parent–child correlations are substantial they are not proof of causation, and several other explanations might be offered to explain why they arise. For instance, similarities may be reported because correlations are based, not upon records of parents' attitudes, but upon children's perceptions of their parents' attitudes. But this apart, it is quite possible that similarities come about because the parental background exposes children to similar sets of values –

through school, through peer contacts and through selective exposure to mass media. If such were the case then it would be unnecessary to evoke a picture of the parents deliberately teaching, or even one in which the parent serves as a model for identification, since it would be sufficient that the child grows up in a particular climate of political opinion and among similarly educated peers.

Much of the work on parent–child transmission has dealt with the early signs of political socialization; there is, however, another major area of discussion of parental influence. Political attitudes among adolescents and adults can be shown to co-vary with other beliefs and values, forming more or less coherent personal ideologies. Knowing a man's views in one area we can often predict with fair accuracy what his views will be on other matters. It seems then, as if some individuals at least possess general characteristics underlying more specific issues which predispose them to view their environments in particular ways.

In the 1950s two exciting and controversial books appeared in which the authors attempted to explore the characteristics of personal ideologies and to explain the origins of individual differences. Eysenck (1954) concentrated upon the organization of attitudes over a wide range of social, moral and political issues and upon the development of a typology. His findings led him to propose that adult's ideologies could be described in terms of two main dimensions of attitudes, one of radicalism–conservatism and the other of toughmindedness–tendermindedness. Using these dimensions, any individual could be placed in one of the four quadrants (e.g. toughminded conservative), and he sought to show that such placings tied in with personality characteristics. Adorno *et al.*'s work (1950) led him to offer a single descriptive dimension for placing individuals, but also more interestingly, to the study of the 'antidemocratic' or potential fascist personality. On this second theme he and his colleagues tried to supplement the usual explanations of ideological stances in terms of direct teaching or exposure to parental views, education and mass media, with the view that the social and political attitudes of some individuals, especially right-wing extremists, are reflections of their personality structure and particular needs. They argued that such individuals were more conventional, more superstitious, less imaginative, more inclined to tough or power solutions to problems, exhibited more destructiveness and cynicism, and were more inclined to aggression towards inferiors and submission to superiors than were liberals. In their personality characteristics, they tended to have more favourable self-impressions, were more punitive towards others and sought to repress or deny their feelings. And, cognitively, they were more rigid in their views, and had a dislike for ambivalence and ambiguity.

A study of some English adolescents (Hebron and Ridley, 1965) gave evidence from a series of pencil-and-paper measures for an association between prejudice scores and self-reports of anxiety and self-esteem. A comparison of mean scores from high and low prejudice groups showed that they differed on self-esteem, esteem for peers and authority figures, anxiety, conventionality, and projective punitiveness, with the more prejudiced consistently underestimating others, highly and rather unrealistically esteeming themselves on good manners and deportment, showing greater anxiety and responding to questions about parental behaviour towards a child in a more punitive manner.

Arguments about the general personality characteristics of authoritarians and non-authoritarians have led to the study of parent–child relationships (e.g. Frenkel-Brunswik, 1948) and to findings, based on reports from children and adults, that home life and relationships are characterized by excessive strictness, rigidity and punitiveness, and by parental rejection and lack of close affectional relationships. Without rejecting the substance of Adorno's descriptions of his subjects, opponents have severely mauled the explanations: it has been pointed out that right-wing authoritarianism correlates inversely with socio-economic status, amount of education and measured intelligence – arguing in effect that the potential fascist arises from educational situations and the social norms of his background rather than from the circumstances of parent–child relations. Some writers have gone even further and questioned the general basis of these 'dimensional' accounts, arguing from their failure to replicate findings that the supposed factors are largely the results of response sets arising from the particular forms of questionnaires used.

It seems unlikely that any one explanation would be adequate to account for variations among ideologies. In most circumstances it seems reasonable to argue for their origins in the family, not through direct teaching but as the result of being born into a particular family in a particular political setting – matters over which the family and the child have little or no control. However, it may well be that the political attitudes of some individuals can be more readily understood if one regards them as expressions of personality characteristics which have been moulded by affectional and authority experiences in childhood – the case can hardly be proved but could be plausible for an extremist element, whatever its political allegiance.

Mass media influences

Television, reading and radio provide such an extensive coverage of political affairs and attitudes that their influence seems inescapable. Children and adolescents are exposed to domestic and international events, to interpretations of present happenings and of the past, to descriptions of other countries and peoples, and to the voices and faces of the political scene. However, it is extremely difficult to determine either the single or the combined effects of mass media. The analysis is complicated in at least three ways. Firstly, the young are selective. This means that much material of direct relevance to politics is ignored (Rutherford, 1966); that 'rational' presentations may be neglected whilst other material of less direct political content but incidentally portraying certain kinds of behaviour, such as in war films, is assimilated; and that one point of view on an issue is over-represented. Secondly, what children read and watch can be influenced by various factors in their background so that it is difficult to determine whether their attitudes stem from the background or the media, or whether these are selectively reinforcing one another or not. Finally, since political attitudes have so many components, some of which are established early and are of an enduring kind, it is likely even in conditions of 'balanced' exposure that some components would be more open to influence than others.

To judge from sales to children and adolescents, weekly comics and magazines can have a widespread influence. Some, like *Robin, Lion, Look and Learn* and *Valentine* each outsell the combined circulations of the *New Statesman,* the *Spectator* and the *Listener.* Such comics contain, in varying degrees, a great deal of material of informative value, present conformist values and behaviour, and light entertainment, but it has frequently been pointed out that they also purvey crude and stereotyped notions of countries and peoples, emphasize nationalistic views of loyalty, sometimes at the expense of other values in human relationships, and in some cases present a great deal of sanctioned violence in the form of war stories. Furthermore, bizarre notions of political leadership are presented. In Superman, for instance, children are presented with a leader possessing supernatural powers who is the saviour of law and order in communities unable to cope with enemies through conventional means – power lying in the hands of an individual who is himself above the law. It is difficult to avoid being absurdly solemn and indignant about comics; nevertheless, at their face value they appear likely to have some undesirable influence, although this may be trivial in comparison to the information and pleasure that many of them give.

There are great differences in content from one comic to another. In a study reported in 1966 Johnson presented a content analysis in terms of mean nationality references and the means for the number of killings and near killings per issue. Three groups of boys' comics were notable in these respects. Educational magazines (e.g. *Finding Out*) were particularly high on nationality references, generally in the context of information articles, but were very low on mentions of killings. Adventure comics, such as *Champion*, and the so-called 'war' comics were very high on both counts, with references to nationality and killings usually occurring in stories about conventional war. Within these last two categories one finds the highly pejorative stereotypes of the traditional Second World War enemies, the morality of goodies and baddies, and the use of violence against the depersonalized enemy. It was among such comics that Johnson found expressions like 'little yellow monkeys', 'rice-eating rats' and 'these Japs aren't human beings'. Some of the American war comics, however, had moved on from Second World War enemies and contained a high incidence of references to communists, 'Commies' and 'Reds'.

Since one of the most salient features of some comics is the unfavourable representation of the 'typical' individual from other countries – commonly in the guise of soldier – Johnson examined associations between reading habits and ethnocentric attitudes, comparing readers and non-readers of war comics. He found that the readers were more ethnocentric, liked other people less (especially Germans, Italians and Japanese), and were less informed about other people. It may be that readers and non-readers were already different in their attitudes and that war comics appealed more to those already prone to unfavourable feelings about others, thus reinforcing rather than forming these attitudes; alternatively the comics could have produced the differences. It must be remembered though that these results were obtained from readers of the most extreme kind of comic and there is no evidence that other kinds have a noticeable connection with children's attitudes. Nor, it should be added, is there any clear evidence on influences from the books that children and adolescents read for pleasure.

The assessment of radio and television influence presents parallel difficulties over the interpretation of associations between attitudes and viewing or listening. Again the case looks strong but the data are inconsistent or simply lacking. Part of the difficulty is that these media are now so well established that the opportunity rarely arises in real-life situations for comparisons to be made between users and non-users. Himmelweit, Oppenheim and Vince's (1958) general investigation of the impact of television upon children, which included political-attitude measures, remains an invaluable source of evidence because it was done in situations where television was relatively, and in one case absolutely, new to the young viewers. Viewers and non-viewers in four English cities were compared and, additionally, data were obtained on children in a city in which television was introduced whilst the survey was in progress. Viewing made children somewhat more interested in other countries, but not significantly so. Attitudes to foreigners were influenced in two ways: they made more objective and fewer statements about them, and they placed more emphasis on describing aspects of foreigners. Also, significantly more viewers than controls disagreed with the statement: 'My own country is always right.' Himmelweit comments that the impact is limited but nevertheless clearly discernible.

Television and comics are probably the more influential sources; children seldom read the political content of newspapers; and radio serves increasingly as background noise. Although the media can influence attitudes, the existing evidence is largely about feelings for and against countries and peoples, and there is little to show whether early orientations to the political system, or conceptual development, are affected. It is possible, for example, that the media increase political awareness and help to make children familiar with a wider range of attitude objects, but these and other effects are likely to be subtle and achieved over a long period.

Education and political attitudes
Education plays such a large part in the lives of the young that one expects it to have a decisive impact upon a wide

range of social and political attitudes. But what effects, if any, does it have? Is it justifiable to conclude, as Hess and Torney (1967), for example, did, that 'the public school appears to be the most important and effective instrument of political socialization in the United States'? Or would it be more correct to say that it generally does no more than to complement other sources of influence – at most confirming what pupils already feel and think, at worst creating a sense of complacency and unreality about politics that leads to mass apathy or outbursts of frustration?

Objectives of political education

Although the content of political education differs from one society to another, and educational institutions are committed to priorities dependent upon the importance attached to them as political agencies, schools, colleges and universities serve three major purposes. They are sources of conservation, helping to create the loyalties and the feelings for participation which are needed either to perpetuate a traditional system or to strengthen a new one. For the most part, conservation is propagandist and only minimally rational. However, system support also rests upon the satisfaction of the political aspirations of influential sectors of society, upon the controlled expression of minority group interests, and upon a supply of reliable and intelligent sponsorship of a pool of children from which a political 'leadership' and a civil service can be drawn, and by raising the general standards of 'good citizenship' across the community. In practice, this means organizing education in such ways as to sponsor élite groups; equally it means providing political instruction which fosters political knowledge right across the community. In part at least, such uses of education indicate concern for greater 'rationality' in citizenship and public service, and an attempt to reduce negative prejudices and inflexibility. It is in this latter area that the political purposes of education are most popularly recognized by teachers and the public, and are explicity revealed in the curriculum in the shape of problem-oriented courses which deal with such diverse matters as intergroup conflict within a society, international 'understanding' and modes of conflict resolution.

Political education in national systems

The ways in which education is used as an instrument of political education and the forms of instruction clearly differ from one society to another. The Soviet Union illustrates those societies where education is consciously directed to political ends. Schools and higher institutions are responsible for presenting a communist viewpoint on national and international affairs, for inculcating love of the motherland, and for developing, through moral and political instruction, an outlook which stresses comradeship, collective activity and responsibility, and loyalty to the Party. A policy statement in November 1958 of the Central Committee of the Communist Party (cited by Grant, 1964) said: 'Upbringing must inculcate in the schoolchildren a love of knowledge and of work, and respect for people who work; it must shape the communist world outlook of the pupils and rear them in the spirit of communist morality and of boundless loyalty to the country and the people, and in the spirit of proletarian internationalism.' Soviet society is obviously not unique in having basic moral-political purposes for education. Non-communist societies, through religious instruction, moral teaching in schools and direct political study, seek to purvey a unified outlook, although of a different kind. What is striking, however, is the way in which Soviet society does the job. State control of all educational institutions, of teaching appointments, and of syllabuses and textbooks ensures that all pupils and students are exposed to a common outlook and have little opportunity to hear or to read anything other than 'official' attitudes. For the younger children there is little formal political instruction, the emphasis being upon the inculcation of attachment to the motherland and its values through exposure to moral precepts, 'school' rules, to tangible symbols of communist leaders and to national events embodied in commemorations. Formal political education is given to older children in the form of approved courses of social studies, and direct teaching on Marxist–Leninist ideology is a component of all forms of higher education (10 to 15 per cent of course time). The impact is further strengthened by the close ties between formal education and the Party youth movement – the Octobrists, Pioneers and *Komsomol* – which not only provides an exhaustive range of leisure facilities for pupils and students but also, depending on the level, exposes them to collective activities, opportunities to exercise leadership, and meetings and rituals which encourage allegiances to motherland and Party.

Political education in non-communist societies varies enormously in its contents, methods and objectives. However, there is commonly a less explicit and organized intent to use the schools as instruments for indoctrination; ideological and partisan teaching is discouraged; and far greater freedom is often given to schools and to individual teachers to design courses and to use textbooks of their choice. Furthermore, there is no compulsory element of political instruction in higher education where it is usual instead to find political debate controlled by students through voluntary societies.

In the USA there is a long tradition, dating back to the early days of the Republic, of civic instruction in the schools, and the great majority of high schools now provide elective courses, particularly in the senior years, which most pupils attend. Civic instruction was initially highly oriented towards creating loyalties to the Republic and towards elementary information on a democratic and republican form of government. Whilst these objectives of 'Americanization' are still present, the over-all scope of courses has increased, especially in the direction of international affairs, so that by the side of courses on American government and problems of democracy one also finds Americanism, communism and democracy, international relations, world citizenship and comparative politics, and contemporary history. Despite the variety of titles, however, courses fall into two major groups, those on American government which focus heavily upon the forms, structures and traditions of government and American public life, and those on 'problems' which range more widely over the disciplines, are wider in subject scope, are more contemporary and are organized around major American problems. Schools typically offer one or the other, and the majority of older students in high school have taken one such course (Langton and Kent Jennings, 1968).

Of the five American and European countries studied by Almond and Verba (1963), England was the only one in which the majority of respondents said that virtually no time was spent in school studying current events and government. Whilst it is probably arguable that our schools have relatively few spots in the timetable marked 'civics', 'current affairs' or 'government', and that direct reference to political objectives rarely appears among the aims of English education, it is absurd to suggest that politics is kept out of the schools. From infancy pupils are taught acceptable ways of conducting their relations with others, they are brought up on nationally biased history and geography, they are exposed to symbols and ceremonies of nationality, and in the process gain in a variety of subtle and not so subtle ways discriminatory notions about the histories, customs and beliefs of other peoples and countries, and their own. Also, in a country such as England, where educational provision is closely associated with both social stratification and mobility, differential exposure to quantity and quality of education and to peer values seems likely to affect partisan and wider outlooks. Finally, in the wider ideological sense, the many links between schools and religious institutions seem likely to foster both positive feelings towards certain religious and moral beliefs and behaviours, and negative attitudes towards groups and societies which reject these or appear to threaten them. Our schools may, of course, do a singularly inefficient job of political education, they may well have quite opposite effects from those they hope to have, but they are certainly agencies for political socialization.

The nature of educational influences

There are several ways in which education may affect political socialization and intergroup attitudes. Instruction itself is an obvious means but, as we shall point out later, the approach depends for its effectiveness upon many factors – knowledge of the children involved, the quality of teaching, and skilled choice of appropriate instructional techniques. Another source of influence lies in the opportunities created by schools and classrooms for bringing individuals together and exposing them to the beliefs, feelings and behaviour of others. Children can contact children and adults from other groups in school and recreational activities, and can be led to participate in community activities. Again, however, qualifications have to be made. Contact alone is not enough; its success depends upon the organization of the situation. Other means lie within educational systems rather than particular schools or teachers. Political decisions and legal enactments can create new opportunities for intergroup contacts, for example, by school desegregation, and can let it be seen that formal discrimination is not sanctioned. Also, the quality of general educational provisions can be raised. Changes within educational systems seem to be particularly important for the long term since they have repercussions across the adult community as well as among the children who draw their attitudes in large part from parents and from prevailing community norms.

In practice, of course, the different resources of education rarely operate in isolation from one another. Indeed, when a particular issue assumes sufficient importance then all available means may be deliberately drawn together in a concentrated effort. Some of the best instances of this have occurred over attempts to assimilate immigrant minorities. Guskin and Guskin (1970) give a fascinating account of methods used to resocialize Chinese pupils in schools in

Thailand. Schools, teachers, older Chinese students and class peers are all employed within a system designed to discourage Chinese identity and to reward adoption of Thai behaviour and language. In this way desocialization and the creation of new identities interacted over the years, with the later reward that if a Chinese became Thai, spoke Thai language as a Thai, and looked and acted like a Thai he was given all the educational and occupational opportunities open to Thais.

Since education offers many ways of influencing pupils, and since it is closely connected with other agencies which may present similar attitudes to those of the school or conspire with it to restrict the views to which pupils are exposed, there would appear to be strong grounds for supposing that it has far-reaching effects. However, it is very difficult to demonstrate empirically what these effects are and one often has to rely upon indirect evidence.

One of the more disquieting forms of evidence comes from adult surveys (e.g. Converse, 1964; Stokes, 1964). These indicate that the mass public is operating at lower levels of information, 'rationality' and efficiency than even the disillusioned observer might suspect. This lack of presumed 'good citizen' characteristics is most marked amongst those who belong to the lower social classes and who have had the least education. If education has had any effects then they appear to have worn off rather quickly and, in any case, such effects as it might have had are not easy to disentangle from social class and measured intelligence. Both in Adorno *et al.*'s original study of the authoritarian personality and in later work, substantial correlations have been reported between socio-economic status, measured intelligence, length of education, ethnocentrism and authoritarianism. Ethnocentrism scores rise as IQ or years of education fall; and authoritarianism, as measured by Adorno's *F* scale, correlates negatively with years of education and IQ (Christie, 1954). The less educated people are the more prejudiced they are likely to be, but the degree of prejudice may have little to do directly with education itself, and there are plenty of actual situations where extensive education on a mass scale exists side by side with highly unfavourable prejudices held by a large sector of the community against another sector.

A more direct approach proceeds on the argument that if education is playing a distinctive part in moulding attitudes then one would expect to find, for example, that, as they grew older, children's attitudes became more like those of their teachers. Hess and Torney (1967) reported a narrowing gap, based upon correlations between such matters as teachers' practices in displaying the American flag and children thinking that the flag symbolizes America. However, as Sears (1968) has pointed out, the various correlations obtained are quite mixed in size and the authors have failed to show that the similarities are specific to teachers rather than to educated adults or adults in general. More research is needed which concentrates on the classroom itself and upon co-variance between the teacher's and the class's attitudes. This would call for kinds of systematic observation and intraclass testing that have not yet been applied.

A further method for assessing school influence draws its conclusions from mass comparison over schools of distinct types of civic education. In doing so it indicates effects that might arise if instruction were made different in presentation and content; it doesn't tell one how influential schools in general are. One of the large-scale American studies of educational programme stemmed from polling done by the Purdue Opinion Poll Panel. Mainer (1963) tested students in high schools across the United States on measures of authoritarianism, social discrimination and ability, then examined the data over a five-month period for shifts in attitudes to discrimination in relation to personal characteristics of students, their environments and whether the schools provided intergroup education programme. Despite the limitations of the gross approach, one gets a valuable impression of the effects of the programme and of the interactions between school, environment and personality of students. Over the five-month period, the scores of students in schools with programmes shifted significantly towards less discriminative attitudes whilst pupils in the other schools showed little change in scores. Beyond this, upper-grade students changed more against discrimination than did younger ones, and more able pupils showed more favourable change. Some cultural-psychological variables interacted with teaching to produce different effects upon attitudes: thus, in schools with such programmes Catholic pupils shifted more against discrimination than did Protestants, but in the other schools the situation was reversed; changes in both kinds of schools were greater amongst Southern pupils than amongst Easterners; and, lastly, highly authoritarian students became more opposed to discrimination in schools with programmes, but actually more favourable to it in the schools without.

Langton and Kent Jennings's (1968) investigation of the impact of high-school civics courses makes depressing reading. High-school seniors in ninety-seven schools were classified according to the number and types of civics courses they had attended and analyses were made of scores on measures of political knowledge, efficacy and cynicism, participation and discussion. Findings for the whole sample showed virtually no differences between those who had not taken courses and those who had taken one or more. Among those who had taken courses there was scant differences between those who had taken the traditional type courses on American government and those who had attended 'problems' courses. Furthermore, when results were examined in relation to students' ratings of courses and teachers, there was no indication of course-quality and interest effects. Only with the small Negro subsample was there any substantial evidence of effects. Here, attendance on courses correlated significantly with political knowledge; those who attended them scored higher on civic tolerance, and they had higher scores on passive loyalty. It seems from the comparison of White and Negro students that the curriculum exerted more influence upon the latter, particularly upon those from less-educated families where the effect was to move them to a position more similar to that of White students. The authors suggest that the shifts among Negroes are due to the exposure, through courses, to information and outlooks which would otherwise be denied them or restricted because of cultural or class barriers; White students, on the other hand, find the courses redundant since they contain material to which they have repeatedly been exposed in other ways in their backgrounds.

The evidence so far cited has come from large-scale surveys of students in existing courses in schools. It requires to be supplemented by findings from more deliberate and controlled experiments on altering aspects of attitudes by instructional methods. Little has been done in this way regarding attitudes towards the political system, but many attempts have been made to minimize prejudice by providing information which will alter beliefs about minorities. Films, broadcasts, intensive courses, discussions and role playing have all been tried and there is no doubt that they can all have some effect (B. Cooper, Mapes and McQuail, 1966; Goldberg, 1956; Hayes and Conklin, 1953; C. Rosen, 1948). However, the inconsistency of findings suggests that any technique has to satisfy a number of conditions in order to be effective, and that whilst erroneous beliefs can be removed other aspects of the attitude are much less likely to be affected. Brief formal courses and one-shot films or broadcasts are largely ineffective – although the occasional film or programme can highlight the problem of a minority in such a way as to jolt the observer. The film, 'Gentleman's Agreement', which dealt with anti-Semitism has this power. Knowledge of one's subjects with regard to their attitudes and motives is important since this may make it possible to stress the desirable, instrumental consequences of a different outlook. The most effective techniques are those which employ intensive discussion or forms of drama and role playing, and where the subjects are given a realistically oriented view of the actual issues and problems, or are made to look at the experiences of the minority. The teacher who has a good relationship with his students and who can communicate his own favourable attitudes, is most likely to be influential. The difficulties in satisfying these conditions in actual school practice are obvious. Teachers are not usually well-informed social psychologists, nor are they always able, either through school circumstances or technical skills, to implement successfully some of the suggested methods. Thus one is forced to return to an issue that affects other fields of teaching skills, the training of teachers.

Higher education is probably the most thoroughly investigated area of all. There are many obvious reasons why it should be an interesting stage. For the student it signifies a break from many of the direct parental constraints and influences; he or she is entering a period in which new subjects will often be taken; the climate of learning and the influences of faculty members will both be rather different from school; and, perhaps most important of all, the student will meet new fellows and make new friends in the context of a distinctive peer community. On the other hand, for the researcher there is the opportunity to study academic élites, able and usually willing to talk about themselves, within the fairly neat confines of three or four years in a particular institution, and of an age when they are able to participate in politics.

Surely here the impact of education can be decisively demonstrated? Unfortunately, studies have often failed to compare changes in attitudes in college or university with changes that may have taken place amongst those who do not attend. Also, many studies have not separated the influences of students' backgrounds from the effects of education; thus, for example, those who enter higher education may be very different from those who do not. Despite these shortcomings the evidence on the whole indicates several important effects and non-effects. Although the better educated are usually better informed on political affairs, higher education does not appear to lead to generally significant improvements in information (McClintock and Turner, 1962), and in some areas of information about local and practical politics the less educated can be as well attuned as the better educated. College and university are often thought of as 'liberalizing' influences in political senses, but there are considerable variations from one institution to another. A study at Cornell University (Goldsen, Rosenberg, Williams and Suchman, 1960) suggested a slight trend from liberal to conservative on such issues as free enterprise, the welfare state and government control. In other American universities similar shifts have been recorded. General shifts within institutions mask differences among students in different departments and faculties: those in social sciences are more liberal than those in most other curricula; engineers, in contrast to students in mathematics and humanities, have been reported as shifting towards conservatism. Partisan flexibility increases, with distinctive rates of defections from different political home backgrounds. At Cornell, where Republicans were in a majority of three to one, the rate of defection from Democratic homes was far greater than from Republican ones, and it was greatest for students whose fathers had political preferences which did not follow the usual partisan patterns for their socio-economic groups. Defection is associated with the ability and the subject study of students; brighter students in the humanities in several institutions show a net shift from Republican to Democrat for men and from Republican to Independent for women (Webster, Freedman and Heist, 1962). Authoritarianism and ethnocentrism usually decline over the college years and graduates also show more tolerance of religious and political heterodoxy than those who have not been to college. Finally, whilst 'impulse expression' increases during college it does not seem that this is associated with greater ideological extremism; in fact, most students become more careful about endorsing extreme statements of all kinds – whether this reflects more tolerance or acquiescence in what is perceived as the proper way for a student to behave when faced with extreme opinions is not really clear.

Of the various stages of education the last most clearly illustrates the importance of non-instructional factors in attitude formation and change. The characteristics of educational systems, of institutions and of student communities rather than of courses and methods of teaching probably represent the really effective levels of influence throughout education and across the whole spectrum of political attitudes. Political scientists, having noted the associations between socio-economic factors and educational variables, are especially interested in the connections between social origins, self- and other selection within education, and differential political socialization. Their arguments assume that socio-educational differences in the treatment of pupils serve both deliberately and unwittingly to conserve the existing political system by exposing individuals to different forms of authority and to distinctive conceptions of the social and political roles of adults, and that the distinctive educational treatment given to some pupils, either because they come from adult élites or are sponsored by selection practices, enables existing political authority to regulate future developments within the political system. On the other hand, social psychologists have generally concerned themselves with the influences of the school or college community, with their peer values and student 'cultures', upon the individual, and with the ways in which pupils and students of differing personalities resolve conflicts between older, often parental, attitudes and those to which they are now exposed in the educational community.

The English educational systems, with independent public schools and with state schools, and with the organization of the latter into selective grammar and non-selective secondary schools, provide fertile ground for research. It has been suggested, for example, that since patterns of authority can vary significantly not only between schools but also between categories of schools, pupils will acquire different notions about leadership, be given different opportunities to participate in 'political' decisions within the schools, and will come out with different views on their political efficacy and how they should exercise their political rights as adults (Abramson, 1967; Almond and Verba, 1963). Abramson tested these ideas against data from English schoolboys attending selective and non-selective schools. Those who had been to a grammar school were more likely to believe that class barriers were being broken down and to identify themselves as middle class. Educationally selected boys had a higher sense of political efficacy and were rather more likely to agree with the statement: 'Only properly educated persons should be political leaders.' However, party preference showed little shift from parental party and the only evidence that educational selection contributes to political disaffection came from the few middle-class boys in non-selective schools. This study, in fact, provides very little evidence for differential socialization arising from educational selection, and such evidence as there is cannot necessarily be ascribed to educational influences since no attempt was made to control for effects of intelligence or for those of home background.

Educational selection can occur at another level. Within schools pupils may or may not be 'streamed' and, where they are, 'streaming' can result in more or less homogeneous social-class groups. Since pupils spend a lot of their time with peers in their own classes, both in the formal and informal school community, the 'streaming' system may affect the values to which pupils are exposed and, in turn, their political attitudes. Langton (1967), in his study of Jamaican children, tried to establish whether homogeneous class peer groups reinforced the political culture of the working class while heterogeneous groups resocialized lower-class pupils in the direction of upper-class norms. Pupils in the two different situations were questioned on their attitude to voting, on civil liberties, on frequency of political discussion and reading, and on political cynicism. Throughout the investigation the results indicated that working-class pupils in heterogeneous class schools and peer groups differed from their counterparts in homogeneous class environments, with the former changing in the direction of higher-class political norms, that is, more democratic attitudes, more support for civil liberties, more positive views on voting and increased economic conservatism. If one takes together the studies of Abramson and Langton and views them in relation to arguments of the effects of comprehensive education, then it seems clear that any effects upon political socialization which might be assumed to arise from comprehensive reorganization would only do so if comprehensive schools were internally 'non-streamed' and had pupil representation across the social classes. The various half measures labelled 'comprehensive' can only be ineffectual. It is, of course, another matter as to whether one wishes to engineer consciously attitude shifts through secondary reorganization, especially towards some upper-class political values such as economic conservatism.

General policies on educational provision, coupled with appropriate internal school organization, can create majority–minority contacts as well as social-class ones. Desegregation policies in school systems in the United States are an outstanding illustration, but one can also add more specific practices like organized recreational and camp facilities, and the introduction of minority-group teachers into schools. But does contact between individuals or groups necessarily lead to a decrease in prejudice?

The implementation of desegregation legislation has provided many opportunities for studying its effects on children. Singer (1964), comparing an all-white school with one in a community which had followed school integration for several years, found that white children in the integrated school had more positive stereotypes of Negroes, had a greater desire for personal contact with them and showed a more positive attitude towards Negro celebrities. However, the white children still placed Negroes low on a social distance scale. Other studies have not been consistent in finding more favourable attitudes. Similar inconsistencies have been found for recreational and camp settings. At best, some favourable changes have occurred; Campbell and Yarrow (1958) found that friendship choices with Negro cabin mates increased, but these attitudes were not applied in other contexts. Introducing a minority-group teacher to give instruction about his country and background can be very effective (James and Tenen, 1953). As we saw with instructional methods, particular factors within the situation play a major part in determining effectiveness, for example, the extent to which teachers can create equal-status conditions and guide children towards common goals, or the choice of a minority-group teacher who is both a skilled instructor and an approachable and like-able person. Yet even when such conditions can be met, key factors in shifts towards more favourable views and in the generalization of the adapted behaviour over many contexts are the attitudes of adults within the community and family, and children's perceptions of such attitudes. If these fail to shift in response to changed school policies then the value of school and other agencies having contact with the child may be severely restricted.

The influence of peers has been most extensively studied among older students in colleges and universities. Several writers (e.g. Coleman, 1965) argue that the larger student 'culture', represented in attitudes to study, sports and student politics, in membership of social and residential groups, and in admiration for those who control role assignments which are important within the adolescent culture (often 'non-academics') is the main educational force at work in reinforcing or changing attitudes. The institutions themselves have virtually no direct instructional effect and, in so far as students are affected by the general academic values, it is to the extent that these are interpreted and then transmitted by the students to new students.

The political views adopted or conserved by students depend, then, upon very complex interactions between academic climate, peer values, student residence or non-residence, actual group membership and aspirations to membership of other groups, initial political attitudes, and the relative pull of background and institution. There is hardly likely to be a clear basis on which to predict how things will go, but there are some useful pointers to the relative importance of factors in particular settings.

One of the classic studies of attitude change in relation to college education was done by Newcomb (e.g. 1965) in the late 1930s when he investigated political attitudes among the student body of Bennington College, Vermont, at that time a small and intensely political college with a liberal faculty much concerned with the events of the period and with acquainting its students with the nature of the contemporary social and political scene. Most students went through marked changes from freshman conservatism to senior non-conservatism. However, despite the strong political climate some individuals changed little or not at all over the years. A simple view of wholesale assimilation into a small and residential community could hardly be supported and it was necessary to take into account both group membership and aspirations, and background pull. A more detailed study of the most conservative and least conservative seniors from three graduating classes showed characteristic patterns of social attitudes and behaviours affecting their political outlooks. Close parental ties, restricted friendships and failure to satisfy the social rather than the academic hopes that they had whilst in college characterized the conservatives; whilst the extreme non-conservatives reflected desires for emancipation from parents, aspirations to college 'leadership' and willingness to conform. Newcomb concluded that 'in a community characterized by certain approved attitudes, the individual's attitude development is a function of the way in which he relates himself both to the total membership group and to one or more reference groups'. A more recent study (Siegel and Siegel, 1957) which investigated shifts in authoritarianism among students in residence in a large university showed that direction and extent of change was determined by students' aspirations towards membership of

particular residences and by subsequent membership of
what had been their reference group (i.e. the group they
aspired to become members of) but not their membership
one. The other pull – that of the parent – and the ways in
which it is handled by individuals has received relatively less
attention apart from such case studies as those by Lane
(1968).

There is little comfort to be taken from these studies of
college students. Attitudes appear to change because of
negative reactions to parents, because of social aspirations,
because of conformist acquiescence – anything, it seems,
rather than positive reappraisal at a 'rational' level.

Political education and the teacher

Looking at research on the development of political attitudes one is struck by the apparent ineffectiveness of teaching. Although the quantity of education is associated
broadly with political knowledge and feelings about a wide
range of attitude objects, and the deliberate use of particular instructional techniques and programmes can result
in significant shifts in attitudes, there is still widespread
ignorance, apathy and irrationality among adults, and
much of the demonstrated influence of schools and colleges can be attributed to sources other than teachers and
instruction, such as peers or socio-educational backgrounds.

The findings are startlingly inconsistent with the influence
that might be assumed to operate through the exposure of pupils and students to highly trained and authoritative people over periods of ten to fifteen years. Part
of the explanation may lie in the very early origins of many
elements of political awareness, emotional attachments to
community and country, and partisan preferences; these
irrational but often highly persistent elements may be
present before teachers exert any considerable deliberate or
incidental influence. The findings may also reflect the failure of research to date to uncover evidence on teacher
influence. If teachers are important in this respect then it

is probably in a cumulative way over the long term, so that individual and brief influences may be too subtle to register. Furthermore, they seem most likely to influence pupils in their main area of expertise, namely the development of intelligence and knowledge. If this is so then their influence would be on pupils' capacities for thinking and not the overt objects of attitudes, and on the subtle processes of concept formation and attainment. These are difficult matters to demonstrate since there is no direct connection between the teacher and the pupils' applications to his political world. Finally, where formal political education is given in the form of civics, modern studies, history and geography teaching, some of the current techniques and curricula may be the least effective ways of going about instruction. Writing on some of the practices in the United States, Newman (1968) said:

By teaching that the constitutional system of the US guarantees a benevolent government serving the needs of all, the schools have fostered massive public apathy. Whereas the Protestant ethic calls for engagement ... the political creed breeds passivity. One need not struggle for his political rights, but only maintain a vague level of vigilance, obey the laws, make careful choices in elections, perform a few duties ... and his political welfare is assured.

He sees current practices giving misleading conceptions of political processes; instruction emphasizes a formal, legalistic view of public affairs or abstract methods and models of inquiry, and minimizes conflicts of values, social injustice, the role of various pressure groups in politics, and the personal ambitions, motives and behaviours of men who form public policies. The consequence of shielding pupils from reality is disillusion and cynicism. A further weakness of current practice is to be found in courses with the objective of fostering 'international understanding'. Pupils are exposed through relatively short courses of glossed impressions of other countries and peoples with the intention of reducing negative prejudices, yet these brief attacks on the affective elements of attitudes are aimed precisely at those points in the pupils' attitude systems that have existed longest and are least susceptible to direct modification. Furthermore, if they are superficially influential it is only to have produced in many pupils a negative acquiescence: new prejudices are exchanged for old.

The apparent limitations of desk-bound formal instruction have already stimulated changes in curricula and teaching techniques. It is increasingly common to find courses which focus upon international conflicts and problems, upon more realistic presentations of political decision making, and upon teaching pupils the use of conventional means to political influence – lobbying, canvassing, campaigning and letter writing (Newman, 1968). Other changes involve breaking out from the classroom in order to give direct observation and participation. Pupils observe local government at work, they visit public services and they are encouraged to do voluntary work programmes. Educational institutions themselves are giving pupils and students greater representation and influence in their administration and policymaking. However, particularly in the area of international affairs, practical involvement is barely possible: here role playing in international 'games' and in crisis simulations has many advocates, especially for teaching older pupils, student teachers and social-science students (Boardman, 1969). In these, the role players are given maps and information on real or fictitious countries, rules governing relationships and behaviour, and positions as politicians, diplomats and military leaders, and then, through the passing of written messages from team to team and the meeting of individual team members, play the 'game', making decisions and developing strategies. Among the advantages claimed for games/simulations are that they help pupils and students to appreciate the complexities of real situations and of human motives and behaviour, that they stimulate critical thinking and argument, and that role playing creates a level of interest across more individuals than is the case for formal instruction.

The common impression among those teachers who use these various techniques is that greater interest is aroused, and that many pupils get a great deal of satisfaction and wider understanding from participation in community affairs. However, where formal evaluation has been attempted (e.g. Cherryholmes, 1966) little clear evidence is available about the effects of such techniques upon attitudes or cognitive skills.

Overview

The political attitudes of adults are in large measure the products of socialization and developmental processes extending back into childhood and adolescence. Basic feelings about nationality, other peoples and countries, and political authority appear first, usually well before children manifest any political knowledge. Partisan preferences are expressed before they are aware of issues, and these preferences, together with feelings about the working of the political system, often show remarkable persistence through to late adolescence and beyond. These initial elements of attitudes are gradually complemented by knowledge and this in turn is regulated by general developments in children's and adolescents' thinking. The effect of increasing cognitive sophistication is to enable the adolescent to apply a 'rational' approach to political affairs; this capability, however, is less in evidence than emotive responsiveness to political problems.

Home, peers, mass media and education represent four major clusters of influences upon both the formation and change of attitudes. Each cluster is connected with the others, and within each the impact upon the individual can come through many processes, such as didactic accumulation of information, parental and secondary identifications, rearing patterns and personality development, and the satisfaction of social needs in group affiliations and conformity to prevailing values. However, research done so far has not given very convincing evidence on some of the assumed processes of transmission of values. Furthermore, it has proved difficult to support some of the claims about the primary importance of this or that agency. For example, there is virtually no evidence of a primary independent effect arising from education, and most of the educational studies indicate that such effects as arise do so from individuals being in educational communities rather than from processes of school or further learning.

Studies of the political attitudes of adolescents and adults generally indicate low levels of political knowledge of all kinds, minimal political participation and considerable apathy and cynicism. Many of the conventional attributes of 'rationality' and 'good citizenship' are lacking. Political socialization seems to have established the basic loyalties and then stopped. Some of the blame is put upon the failure of the schools to present a realistic and problem-oriented view of political affairs, leading perhaps to cynicism and apathy or to illegitimate and sometimes violent protest when the young adult is exposed to the realities of adult politics. Schools have also been blamed for restricting pupils' exposure to diverse attitudes through selection and 'streaming' practices. In fact, much of the blame must lie within the political system itself in that it commonly offers relatively few incentives for political expression to the mass of young adults. However, the relative ineffectiveness of education, especially in areas of political knowledge, suggests that more might be done. Teachers themselves could be more fully instructed on the processes and patterns of political development so as to make their teaching more appropriate; much more realism could be brought into the curriculum through active discussion of political problems in place of doses of colourless information; political role playing could supplement direct instruction and discussion; and more use might be made of opportunities for school–community projects. Research into the effectiveness of such procedures is often lacking, but the practical experiences of individual teachers suggests that they might be worthwhile.

4 Education and Occupational Choice

In chapter 1 it was suggested that the nature and length of a person's formal education, and the academic success which he achieves through it, are important factors in determining the socio-economic status of his adult occupation. But education may also be relevant to occupations and careers in other ways. Since it is generally accepted that a major concern of schools should be the preparation of pupils for their adult roles as workers, one may hypothesize that educational experiences affect the kind of occupations which people choose.

Occupations have been classified in many ways, but there is general agreement on the value of a two-way classification according to level and type. The level of an occupation is closely related to socio-economic status. Roe (1956), whose system has been one of the most widely used, differentiated six levels according to 'the degree of personal autonomy and the level of skill and training required'. In this chapter, however, it is with the factors influencing the choice of types of occupation within any level that we shall largely be concerned. There is far less agreement as to how occupations can most usefully be classified into types, but the general sort of distinctions with which we shall be concerned may be exemplified by Roe's system; in this, occupations are further classified into eight groups according to 'the primary focus of activity in the occupation'. These are (Roe, 1956, pp. 145–7):

Service: serving and attending to the personal tastes, needs and welfare of other persons, e.g. medical practitioner, domestic help.
Business contact: face-to-face sale of commodities, services, etc., e.g. auctioneer, sales representative.

Organization: organization of commercial enterprises or government activities, e.g. manager, civil servant.

Technology: production, maintenance and transportation of commodities and utilities, e.g. civil engineer, plumber, truck driver.

Outdoor: cultivation, preservation or gathering of natural resources, e.g. farmer, miner.

Science: scientific theory and its application (other than technology), e.g. research psychologist, laboratory technician.

General culture: preservation and transmission of the general cultural heritage, e.g. school teacher, journalist.

Arts and entertainments: use of special skills in the creative arts and entertainment, e.g. composer, comedian.

Any such simple classification of occupations must necessarily be somewhat arbitrary, but Roe's system, which in general reflects the way in which people's interests have been found to vary, does serve to demonstrate some of the fundamental ways in which occupations differ irrespective of their level or status.

How far are choices among such different types of occupation affected by factors associated with education? There are, it may be suggested, three major ways in which educational experience may be relevant to occupational decision making:

1. Because of perceived relationships between subjects studied at school and occupations, preferences among school subjects, or aspects of subjects, may be extrapolated to preferences among occupations; or tentative occupational choices may be tested against experience of apparently related subjects.

2. Decisions, made and implemented during the course of one's education, to follow specialist courses of study may limit the range of occupations which one is qualified to enter, or for which one is qualified to train.

3. Information acquired in the course of one's education about the nature of occupations, about career opportunities, and about oneself, together with advice given by teachers or counsellors, may influence both the process of making a decision and the occupation decided upon.

The relevance of education can best be considered, however, in the context of a wider view of the processes and factors involved in occupational choice. We shall first, therefore, look at some of the ways in which social scientists have attempted to describe and explain various aspects of occupational choice. Following this, we shall consider the development of preferences and choices between school subjects in the context of the British educational systems, with, therefore, particular emphasis upon the choice between specialization in arts or science subjects. The final section of the chapter will deal with the influence of information and advice on occupational choice, with particular regard to the influence of school and other official personnel.

The process of occupational choice

An individual's entry into an occupation is the outcome of a complex process of interaction between the characteristics of the individual and those of the society in which he lives. It depends both upon the individual's hierarchy of choices among various occupations and upon a selecting agency's hierarchy of choices among various individuals. These hierarchies of choice are not, however, independent of one another, since the choices must be assumed to result from some sort of compromise between what the individual or institution would prefer and what they perceive they are likely to succeed in obtaining. Thus at the point of attempted entry there are complex relationships between the individual's characteristics, those of the occupation and the people who control entry into it, and the ways in which others perceive the individual. But even before this point has been reached, the development of an individual's occupational preferences and choices is a process in which, at every stage, social experiences not only influence the individual's personality and abilities, but also influence his perception of the occupational implications of his own characteristics.

In so far as it is possible to separate the two, it is with the processes of choice rather than with those of selection that we are concerned. Even with this restriction, however, the number and variety of questions to be asked is considerable. They may perhaps be grouped under four main heads:

1. In what ways do people who seek different types of occupation differ in their personal characteristics and how are these relevant characteristics inter-related?
2. In what ways do people who seek different types of occupation differ in their past experiences and how are these past experiences related to personal characteristics?
3. Can any general patterns be discerned in the processes by which occupational preferences develop with age and experience?
4. How do people eventually come to decide upon an occupation, or a specific position, to which they will attempt to gain entry?

Personality characteristics

Much research into occupational preference and choice has been based on the common-sense notion that the jobs which people find congenial, and therefore those which they choose to enter, vary according to their personal characteristics. What, it is asked, are the distinctive traits of people who choose to become, for example, teachers, dentists or shop assistants?

The most obvious way to seek answers to these questions is to investigate people's interests. From the hypotheses that people prefer to earn a living doing things they like doing, and that jobs are chosen with some knowledge of the activities they involve, it follows that people choosing different jobs should differ systematically in their interests. Extensive investigations, notably those of Strong (1943), have confirmed that this is the case. Such interoccupational differences, however, are not generally large in comparison with variation of interests within any one occupation; and there is a high measure of agreement among most people, irrespective of occupation, about the relative attractiveness of different activities.

The relation between interests and occupations might result from, rather than be caused by, commitment to occupations or involvement in the different activities they require. Such alternative explanations would be consistent with findings that interests tend to be relatively unstable until the late teens. Evidence from several studies, however, suggests that vocational interests are not affected by occupational experience, whether or not this experience is in an occupation consistent with the interests expressed.

Factor analytic studies of occupational interests within different populations and assessed by various techniques, have produced remarkably consistent results. Much of the variation among people can be described in terms of the following dimensions of interest: in people and their welfare, in science, in business or administrative detail, in the use of language, in machines, in physical activity, in aesthetic pursuits and in persuading people. Occupations have been classified according to the patterns of interests, in terms of these dimensions, which most typify their members; and in vocational guidance, much emphasis has been placed on ensuring that an individual's profile of interests is similar to that typical of people in occupations which he is considering.

Consistent differences have been found between the sexes in their occupational interests, both in terms of the extent of their interest in several areas and, more fundamentally, in the pattern of variations in interests within each sex. Sex differences are observable from an early age; Tyler (1951), for example, found significant differences among children in their first year at primary school on such interests as helping adults with work (female interest) and paper-pencil-crayon activity (male interest). Although factor analytic studies of female populations have indicated that some dimensions of interest variation are similar for men and women, women have been found to be most clearly differentiated, not in these terms but in terms of their relative interest in, on the one hand, careers in general and, on the other, domestic duties and family life. While it is probable that careers and family life have seemed increasingly compatible to women during the last thirty years, relatively recent evidence suggests that occupational interests are still relatively unimportant to the majority of women; and that this is so even amongst those who spend several years in training for such professions as teaching and nursing. F. Davis and Oleson (1965), for example, found that over 87 per cent of their sample of student nurses attached more importance to women's 'home and family' role than to their 'work and career' role.

Interest in occupations and careers thus tends to be considerably greater amongst men than women. Does this imply that career-oriented women tend to be generally more like men in their interests and motivations than are other women? Available evidence indicates that no such generalization can be made. Thus it was found in one study of college students that career-oriented women were like men in that they were less likely than other women to rate relations with people as an important aspect of a job; but they were unlike men in that, whereas men were less likely than women to rate self-expression as important, career-oriented women attached more importance to self-expression than other women. Particularly interesting is a longitudinal study by Tyler (1964). She selected two groups of twelfth-grade girls, differentiated on the Strong Vocational Interest Inventory as having career and non-career profiles, and compared the development of their interests from the first grade onwards. In grade 1, those in the career group had made significantly more masculine choices but by the eighth grade it was difference in vocational interests, and not differences on the masculine–feminine dimension, which distinguished the two groups.

Study of interest differences has revealed that people vary in a number of ways in the sort of occupations they find attractive; a parallel body of research has been devoted to the identification of concomitant differences in personality among people choosing different occupations. Most of this research has been conducted with student subjects, taking as criteria not the occupations in which people are actually engaged, but, in order of increasing remoteness from this, involvement in courses of occupational training, occupational preferences and scores on interest inventories. The last two of these have some advantage in that they measure attitudes relatively uncontaminated by factors which might limit freedom of choice; on the other hand, responses to paper-and-pencil questionnaires have far from perfect validity as indicators of a person's actual choice of occupation.

There is a substantial body of evidence showing that people in different occupations tend to differ in their abilities. Such differences, however, could be the result of selection processes or of experience in the occupation. Furthermore, most of the evidence demonstrates relationships between people's general abilities and their occupational choice levels rather than between distinctive aptitudes and types of occupation. A large-scale study which exemplifies the best research in this area as well as some of the major problems is that of Thorndike and Hagen (1959). They compared the aptitude profiles obtained in tests during the Second World War of over 10,000 men who had later entered 124 different occupations, thus minimizing the risk that the associations that they found between occupations and abilities could result from training while in the occupation. The greatest differences between the various occupational groups were in their scores on general ability tests, and a general tendency was found for groups superior on these tests to be superior also on other tests. There were, however, exceptions to this general trend: carpenters, for example, were well above average on mechanical tests but well below average on tests of general intellectual ability. It was not possible to determine the relative influence of individual's own choices and of institutional selection processes in producing these interoccupational differences.

For most people initial occupational choices are made

during, or on completion of, their formal education in school or college. It is, therefore, to a large extent in terms of the perceived relevance of school subjects to various occupations that assessed abilities are likely to influence occupational interests and choices. We return to such influences in a later section of this chapter.

An apparently reasonable hypothesis is that individual differences in *needs* will influence choice of occupation. Thus, for example, people with a high need for affiliation might tend to choose occupations which provide extensive opportunities for warm and friendly social contact, and those with a high need for autonomy might be most often found in occupations allowing freedom for independent action. Indirect support for this thesis comes from investigations such as that of Walsh (1959). He described several duties, each postulated to satisfy a different need, involved in each of several jobs, and found that the duties which students selected as being most and least attractive in the various jobs were related, as he had predicted, to their dominant needs, assessed by a personality questionnaire. Most research in this area, however, has been vitiated by too much reliance on interest questionnaires as opposed to actual choice behaviour, and by difficulties in predicting what needs are likely to be most satisfied in specific occupations.

Another way in which personal needs have been hypothesized to be relevant to occupational choice is with regard to the relative effects on choice processes of the need for achievement and of the need to avoid failure. Atkinson (1957) predicted that people in whom need for achievement is dominant will choose goals which, while attainable, involve the possibility of failure; those more concerned with avoiding failure will minimize risks by setting either easy or impossibly high goals. Applied to occupational choice, this hypothesis has received support from several investigations; in particular, need for achievement tends to be associated with the choice of jobs of higher prestige than those which people fearing failure tend to choose. Risk-taking behaviour, however, appears to influence not only the level but also the type of occupation chosen. Ziller (1957), for example, found that students who manifested the highest level of risk-taking behaviour in an experimental situation were most likely to be interested in sales occupations; at the other extreme, students who took fewest risks tended to be undecided in their occupational plans.

Values are perhaps even more obviously relevant to occupational choice than needs, since they represent the concerns by which people explicitly or implicitly direct their lives. In so far as occupational choice involves goal-oriented behaviour, they would seem to be of central importance. At least so far as occupations of relatively high status are concerned, research results are consistent with this suggestion. (Lower status occupations probably allow less opportunity for the implementation of personal values; but since research has been concentrated on college students, it is not possible to confirm whether this is the case.) An investigation which is fairly typical in its approach, but unusual in the size of the sample studied, is that of Rosenberg (1957). He questioned several thousand students at one American university as to the reasons for their educational–occupational choices. Three basic values were identified which accounted for much of the variation between individuals and which differentiated between groups studying different subjects: (a) prestige and financial concerns, found mostly among students in business studies and least among social work, teaching and natural science students; (b) helping, and working with, people, found mostly among students working in social service fields, e.g. teaching, medicine, and least among science and technology students; and (c) an opportunity for creativity and the use of special talents, found most among students in aesthetic subjects and least among those in business subjects. Changes in either expressed values or subject fields over a period of two years tended to bring individuals more into line with these general patterns. Results consistent with these have emerged from several other studies.

Many other personality characteristics have been investigated in relation to occupations or occupational preferences. By compounding results from different investigations, one may tentatively suggest what distinctive characteristics members of specific occupations tend to have (see Osipow, 1968, pp. 182–93). Thus engineers, for example, tend to be interested in things rather than people, to be orderly, not introspective, unimaginative, emotionally stable, and to be both authoritative and ready to accept the authority of others. Teachers tend to be socially oriented in their interests and values, to be relatively low in need for achievement, to be rather conformist and to enjoy identifying with groups. But it must be emphasized that the smallness of interoccupational differences in comparison with intraoccupational variations means that any but the most cautious use of such generalizations is likely to be dangerously misleading. Furthermore American findings about specific occupations, such as those summarized above, cannot with confidence be extrapolated to other national cultures.

Some personality theories of occupational choice depend on the assumption that people are well informed about the occupations they choose. Holland (1966), in contrast, has developed a theory which accepts and utilizes the common finding that people perceive the vocational world in terms of crude occupational stereotypes. Since stereotypes of occupations are widely shared, the ways of life people prefer can be coded in terms of these shared stereotypes. He therefore constructed a Vocational Preference Inventory to assess people's various personal orientations in terms of their reactions to 300 different occupations. This is thus a personality theory expressed in terms of occupational stereotypes. People are categorized according to the relative strength of six types of personal orientation: realistic (preferring physical to interpersonal or verbal activities), intellectual, social, conventional, enterprising and artistic. These six types of personal orientation develop differentially in individuals in response to different aspects of the environment, aspects which are reflected in the occupational world. Thus Holland distinguished six types of occupational environment corresponding to the types of personal orientation, having assumed that, while one individual's perception of any one occupation may be seriously distorted, the general stereotyped classifications of occupations tend to be valid. A person manifesting, for example, a predominantly intellectual orientation will tend to choose, and to find satisfaction in, one of those occupations classified as providing a predominantly intellectual environment.

The research conducted by Holland and his colleagues has provided impressive support for this theory. Substantial relationships, generally consistent with those predicted, have been found between scores on the Vocational Preference Inventory and those on several other personality scales, thus not only validating the VPI, but also allowing increasingly sophisticated differentiation among people with different types of profile on it. Personal orientations have been found to be stably and systematically related to the non-vocational activities in which people engage, and also to their choices of career. Stability of career choice has been shown to be greater where choice is consistent with the high point of the profile than where it is not. One major limitation of this research is that the population studied has been a highly selected group of very able students; but research designed to test aspects of the theory with less selected populations (e.g. Osipow, Ashby and Wall, 1966) has obtained results mostly consistent with it.

Personal background and occupational choice

What are the origins of interpersonal differences in occupational preference and choice? Attempts to identify and explain relationships between personal background and occupational choice have focused attention on the influence of the home and particularly relationships with parents. Relationships with parents, especially in infancy, may have a permanent influence on aspects of personality relevant to occupational choice. In addition, choice may be more directly affected by the home, by its influence on occupational values, by the nature and amount of occupational information available to the individual, by direct advice and by the limitations of family approaches to deciding upon an occupation.

Child-rearing practices, personality and occupational choice. Relations between these variables are close to the central concern of psychoanalytic theories and several studies have attempted to test hypotheses derived from such theoretical frameworks. In most cases, the influence of childhood experiences has been inferred from indirect evidence. Nachmann (1960), however, compared law, social work and dentistry students' memories of their family background. By considering the work required in the three occupations, she predicted certain differences in personality and, therefore, in childhood experiences between these groups. For example, the role of the social worker she perceived as not permitting aggressive behaviour of any sort, whereas dentistry, by contrast, she saw as necessarily involving physically aggressive behaviour. She predicted that the social workers would have come from families in which aggressive impulses tended to be accepted more than in families of those who became dentists. Data from interviews with the students supported this and most of Nachmann's other predictions, such as those with regard to the role of fathers and the most rewarded types of behaviour during the pre-school years. Although retrospective reports may have distorted memories of early experiences in ways systematically related to current life-styles, Nachmann's findings suggest the potential value of psychoanalytic theory for relating career choice to patterns of child rearing.

One process proposed by psychoanalysts which is particularly relevant to occupational choice is that of identification. The hypothesis that the development of interests is influenced by the degree of identification with one or other parent has received some empirical support in that expressed interests have generally been found to differ according to whether people have identified more with their fathers or their mothers, and according to the degree of this identification. Thus identification processes appear relevant to career choice in so far as the learning of sex roles is involved; but no direct relationships have been demonstrated.

Roe (1957) theorized that the type of occupation a person chooses is influenced by his dominant psychological needs, and that these in turn depend upon the nature of his childhood experiences. In particular, Roe suggested that needs that are routinely satisfied do not become unconscious motivators; that higher-order needs (e.g. for love, for knowledge) will disappear entirely if they are only rarely satisfied, but that lower-order needs (e.g. hunger) which are rarely satisfied become dominant motivators; and that an important variable affecting whether different needs become important motivators is the typical amount of delay before each is satisfied. The major distinction made by Roe is between person-oriented people, who are most likely to come from loving or overprotective homes, and those who are not person-oriented, and who are likely to have had parents who tended to avoid or reject them.

Roe's theory is particularly impressive in that, while general, it is formulated with sufficient precision to allow most aspects of it to be empirically tested. The findings of research, however, have been fairly consistent in their lack of support for the theory. Hagen (1960), for example, related retrospective information about the child-rearing practices of the parents of university students to the occupations in which these students later become established. Detailed predictions from the theory about associations between types of childhood climate and occupational groups were, with only one exception, unsupported: nor was there any support even for the prediction that those in 'person-oriented' occupations would have reported different parental practices from those in occupations not so oriented.

Roe and Siegelman (1964) carried out a detailed study to assess an extended version of the theory. Major hypotheses were confirmed in that person-orientation was found to be positively correlated with scores on a *loving–rejecting* factor for mother's behaviour, scores on an *overattention* factor for both parents' behaviour, and amount of early social experience. Predictions about occupational preferences and choice, however, were not confirmed. Roe and Siegelman concluded that relations between child-rearing practices and occupational choice are unlikely to be found because of the many intervening variables.

Direct parental influence on occupational choice. In a study involving over 76,000 males entering 246 American four-year colleges, Werts (1968) found a strong tendency for students to enter their fathers' occupations or occupations closely related to those of their fathers. About 35 per cent of the sons of physical scientists chose careers in physical science, compared with 10 per cent and 14 per cent of the sons of medical practitioners and social scientists respectively; and similar patterns were found for all occupations considered. Evidence on a comparable scale is lacking for occupations of lower status and for other countries, but findings with more limited samples suggest that similar tendencies occur in most contexts, although the strength of these tendencies appears to vary considerably; occupational inheritance is indeed more likely to occur where families have made large capital investments, or in isolated and specialized communities (e.g. farming, mining) than with occupations to which entrance is dependent on educational qualifications.

Among the factors which contribute to this tendency are likely to be the influence of the home environment on the adolescent's occupational values, the restricted range of occupations with which he has contact through his home, and the limitations which his parents' own experience and interests impose upon the advice they give him. With regard to the first of these, Kinnane and Pable (1962) classified home environments on the basis of a biographical inventory and related these to the expressed work values of sixteen to eighteen year olds. They found systematic and largely predictable relationships between the two sets of variables; for example, emphasis of 'social-artistic' values was related to the amount of cultural stimulation in the home, and 'security-economic-material' values were associated with homes having materialistic atmospheres.

That the advice and information provided by parents is more influential than that provided from any other sources has been a consistent finding of many investigations (e.g. Carter, 1962; Jahoda, 1952). In giving advice, parents appear to focus their attention upon the characteristics of occupations, putting little emphasis on the interests or personalities of their children. The nature and amount of advice offered tends to vary with social class, middle-class parents generally being more positive in suggesting the sort of work they consider suitable; working-class parents are likely to be less prescriptive, being authoritative about jobs to be rejected but leaving a considerable freedom of choice to their children. Carter (1962) commented that many of the working-class parents in his sample feared lest they would be blamed by their children later for giving wrong advice, but had no worries about being blamed for providing inadequate guidance.

Underlying many of the social-class variations in job-seeking behaviour, and in the parental advice associated with it, are fundamentally different attitudes to work: whereas the middle classes tend to think in terms of *careers* and to emphasize both the intrinsic satisfaction to be gained from work and the importance of ascending an occupational hierarchy, working-class people more commonly think in terms of *jobs,* in which the best one can hope for is security, respectability and pleasant interpersonal relationships. Where this (generally realistic) attitude is taken, the particular activities involved are not seen to be of prime importance, and since changes of job will involve horizontal rather than vertical movement they can be undertaken much more easily; thus while obtaining a job is important, the selection of a job may not be.

The development of occupational choice

In recent years much emphasis has been placed on the idea that the choice of occupations or careers can only be properly understood as a gradual process starting in childhood and not completed for many people until they reach their mid-twenties. Particularly influential in this respect have been the theories of an interdisciplinary group led by Ginzberg (Ginzberg, Ginsburg, Axelrod and Herma, 1951) and of Super (1953), both studies suggesting that there are several developmental stages through which people go before coming to a stable choice.

Ginzberg and his colleagues postulated three main periods in this development: the fantasy period, during which children take no account of reality factors in their occupational 'choices'; the tentative period, approximately between the ages of eleven and eighteen, during which adolescents take account, in the preferences they express, of their interests, abilities and values, in that order, and then of external factors; and the realistic period, during which individuals are usually engaged in occupations or in preparation for occupations, which involves first a reality-testing exploratory stage, then a crystallization of choice and, finally, the specific choice of a specialism or a job. Super's system, in many respects similar, differs in that it takes account of the total life-span and describes crystallization as occurring earlier, generally between the ages of fourteen and eighteen, in the context of vocationally relevant educational decisions (Super, Stavishevsky, Matlin and Jordaan, 1963). Super does not specify the order in which personal characteristics become relevant, but lists a number of attitudes and behaviours necessary before crystallization can occur, including awareness of the need to crystallize, awareness of present–future relationships and of contingencies which may affect goals, differentiation of interests and values, and possession of information about the preferred occupation.

According to Super, the central process in career choice is the development and implementation of an individual's *vocational self-concept*. Self-concepts are developed during childhood and adolescence through the differentiation of one's own characteristics from those of others and through the complementary process of identification with adult models. Vocational self-concepts, which may be more or less integrated with a person's other concepts of himself, vary in their clarity, refinement, stability and realism. Development of an adequate vocational self-concept is especially dependent on the effectiveness with which the adolescent's exploratory behaviour, such as occupational role playing and seeking for information about his academic abilities, provides vocationally relevant information which he can accept. Among factors which hypothetically affect the value of the information are whether or not this exploratory behaviour is self-initiated, purposeful and active, and whether the adolescent is sufficiently non-defensive to be prepared to modify his previous images of himself in the light of dissonant information. Another important aspect of this development of 'vocational maturity' is the translation of relevant beliefs about self into occupational preferences, through the matching of self-concepts with information or beliefs about possible occupations.

Super's theory has the merit that, instead of the assumption that people tend to be drawn by unspecified processes into occupations which suit their personalities, it sees occupational choice as a deliberate activity based upon what people believe to be the realities of the situation; the appropriateness of the choice is then postulated to vary with the validity of these beliefs. This has the additional advantage that it makes possible a specification of the sorts of behaviour on the part of teachers, parents and counsellors which could lead to more adequate choices. For example, children of parents who encourage independence and provide emotional support are more likely to be able to make positive use of information dissonant with their existing self-concepts.

Much of the research aimed at demonstrating the centrality of self-concepts in career development has 'tested' the theory only on the undemanding criteria that occupational preferences should be consistent with self-concepts. Oppenheimer (1966), for example, found a positive correlation between liberal-arts students' rankings of occupations according to preference and the rankings based on degree of agreement between self- and occupational concepts. Where more demanding tests have been made, results have tended to be ambiguous. Warren (1961) assessed discrepancies between self-concepts and intended occupational roles of college entrants, predicting that the greater the discrepancy the more likely it was that a student would change his field of study. This hypothesis was not supported, although students with the greatest discrepancies were found to be more likely than others to make more than one change.

Most research on vocational self-concepts has been concerned with the match between individuals' beliefs and their beliefs about the personalities of typical members of occupational groups. A relatively neglected but potentially salient aspect of vocational self-concepts is a person's assessment of himself in terms of the abilities which he believes necessary for the success in an occupation. M. Rosen (1961) investigated this aspect in a controlled laboratory experiment. Adolescent boys were given false information, supposedly based on the results of an aptitude test, about their chances of gaining entry into occupations. This led to systematic changes in their ratings of the attractiveness of these occupations. For example, of those who were told that they had little chance of entering an occupation which they had rated as highly attractive, 50 per cent lowered their ratings; and 91 per cent of those told they had a very good chance of entering an occupation to which they were previously neutral rated that occupation as more attractive.

A related area of research deriving from developmental theories is that concerned with the stages of development and with the growth of vocational maturity. Super and Overstreet (1960), postulating five dimensions of vocational maturity, assessed ninth-grade pupils (aged about fifteen) in New York on several instruments appropriate to each of the dimensions. Analysis of correlations between scores, however, indicated only two major dimensions. The more important of these, general competence in making decisions, was associated with such variables as general intelligence, school attainment, socio-economic status and vocational aspirations. Since this cluster of variables is that typically associated with the 'successful' pupil, the need to distinguish the growth of vocational maturity from cognitive development in general appears questionable. The second dimension, use of available resources in coping with decision making, was not related to any of the other personal or environmental variables studied.

Other investigators have found that expressions of occupational preferences by ninth-grades are based very largely on interests or simple affective responses, and that the best predictors of the choices which they later implement are their interests and expressed preferences. By the age of eighteen, however, more concern is expressed for social values, information about careers and practical opportunities. While this evidence is generally in accord with developmental hypotheses, some findings have thrown doubt on the detailed suggestions made by the Ginzberg group with regard to the ages at which account is usually taken of different factors. On the one hand, concern with reality factors and values has been found at much younger ages than they predicted; on the other, the influence of interests, although increasingly supplemented by that of other factors, has been reported as remaining dominant throughout the adolescent years and up to the point where choices are crystallized and acted upon.

O'Hara and Tiedemann (1959) set out to test the Ginzberg theory in terms of the accuracy of pupils' self-concepts. They compared the self-ratings, made by boys in grades 9 to 12 of one school, of their interests, aptitudes, values and social class, with objective measures of the same characteristics. Correlations for social class were lowest and remained much the same over the four years; for interests, the correlation rose between grades 9 and 10 and then remained relatively constant; for work values, in contrast, the correlation was stable over the first three years, but was significantly greater in grade 12; for aptitudes, the correlation increased steadily throughout the four years. In general, these results indicate an increasing realism and clarification in pupils' self-concepts during the high-school years; more particularly, they provide partial support for the Ginzberg theory in suggesting that adolescents tend to achieve a maximum awareness of their own interests two years before they focus their attention on their values.

A question of obvious importance is at what stage in his career does the individual crystallize his occupational self-concepts? Stephenson (1961) asked whether this occurred before or after students applied for entry to a medical school. Reasoning that persistence in a field despite rejection indicated a clear and stable self-concept, he studied a large sample of rejected applicants to a school and found that, several years later, two-thirds of them were in medical or medically related occupations. While Stephenson's reasoning may be questioned, this study is important as one of the few attempts to relate career development theory to the choice points which are determined, not by the motivation of individuals, but by educational and occupational structures.

The decision-making process

Although preferences, occupational self-concepts and understanding of the occupational world may develop gradually over many years, there are points in time at which definite decisions have to be made. How these decisions are made is a question with which hardly any empirical research has been concerned. In recent years, however, it has attracted increasing theoretical attention.

Gelatt (1962) has developed a model for describing the pattern of behaviour which he considers would be involved in 'good' occupational decision making. Having specified what decision had to be made, the individual would determine on the basis of the available information (a) what courses of action were open to him, (b) what possible outcomes each of these courses had, (c) the probability of each of these outcomes from each course of action and (d) the desirability of each of the possible outcomes. On this basis he would decide what action to take or what further information he would need before making a decision. This prescriptive model was intended to provide a basis for occupational counselling, and Gelatt did not suggest that it describes the way in which people normally behave.

One attempt to describe the way in which people actually behave in making occupational decisions was made by Hilton (1962). He suggested that decisions are derived from an initial set of beliefs or premises. These may be self-perceptions, felt needs, values, perceived attributes of occupational roles, beliefs about occupational opportunities and about the relative benefits to be gained from different occupations, or feelings about one's present state or situation. Decision-making behaviour is initiated by a stimulus from outside, such as the offer of a job or the approach of the closing date for college entry applications. Arising from this stimulus or from one's premises, tentative plans are formulated. These are judged as satisfactory or unsatisfactory on each of the criteria implicit in the decision maker's premises. If there is a conflict between two or more plans, or if the most favoured plan is dissonant with some of the premises, the decision maker examines his premises and, if possible, changes or adds to them in the attempt to reduce this dissonance. If the premises are not sufficiently changeable, he searches for occupational alternatives and selects a new tentative plan. The plan eventually decided upon is the first one to be formulated which is not dissonant with any premises. Unconscious motivations and feelings not made explicit in a person's premises are important in influencing the order in which alternatives are considered and the effort made to revise premises to make certain plans less dissonant with them. Conditions hypothesized to affect the amount of dissonance experienced include the number and heterogeneity of perceived alternatives, and exposure to a demanding or threatening environment.

The above two models may be viewed as different approaches to the practical goal of being able to help students to adopt improved decision-making strategies. Models such as Hilton's involve a longer term approach since they require to be submitted to empirical investigation. But although the present authors agree with Gelatt's suggestion that the criteria for judging the merits of a decision should be in the process whereby it is reached rather than in the outcome, we believe that an understanding of the processes actually used is more likely to increase the helpfulness of counsellors than the positing of ideal models which bear little relation to normal behaviour.

Occupational choice is not, however, determined by a single once-for-all decision. The usual pattern is rather one of successive decisions over a period of several years. The type of secondary school to attend, the subjects in which to specialize, how long to remain in school, the type of further education, if any, one should embark on: these are some of the decisions commonly involved in occupational choice before any decision committing one to a specific job. Each decision tends to decrease the number of occupations to which a person is likely to obtain entry. Furthermore, as Hershenson and Roth (1966) suggested, successive decisions may narrow the range of occupations to which a person gives consideration, and strengthen the attractiveness of occupations within this range. This would result from adaptations to increasingly specialized conditions; from ignorance of other possibilities and from a tendency to structure one's ideas and perceptions to make them consistent with one's earlier decisions, thus reinforcing one's belief in the correctness of these decisions. In consequence, restrictions on an individual's freedom of choice may be much greater than those imposed by external conditions.

Overview

Despite the large amount of research which has been conducted into occupational choice, only a small proportion of which has been indicated here, there are many aspects of the subject about which we remain ignorant. One limitation of the research is that most of it has aimed to identify distinctive characteristics of people who have chosen, or who express preferences for, particular occupations. The relevance of results from even the best-designed of these studies is limited not only to the specific occupations considered, but also to the contexts in which the choices have been made; yet the processes by which choices are made have generally been ignored by such studies, and the lack of a coherent theoretical framework has made the description of potentially relevant contextual factors impossible. A second limitation has been the concentration of research on college students, and therefore on middle-class youth, and on males.

The major current theories of occupational choice themselves leave several important gaps. Among recent criticisms of these theories (Tennyson, 1968) have been: the neglect of cognitive processes; the concentration on positive attitudes to occupations to the neglect of avoidance behaviour; the neglect of the sudden shifts in occupational preferences commonly observed in young people, particularly those from working-class backgrounds; and the lack of attention given to cultural and situational determinants of choice, such as secondary-school curricula. This last point appears particularly important. As Osipow (1968, p. 235) puts it: 'It has become increasingly evident that when the situational determinants of career development are ignored, serious limitations are imposed on theoretical endeavours. In order to avoid limiting the impact of theory to this time and place, situational factors must be systematically built into career development theory.' In view of this warning, caution should be exercised in generalizing the more specific components of the theory and research summarized here, almost all of which is American, to Britain or other countries.

Choice of school subjects

For many young people, choice of an occupation is to a large extent implicit within the educational choices they make. The nature and timing of the occupationally relevant educational decisions which are made by, for, or about pupils varies widely between and within countries according to the way in which secondary education is organized. In Britain, major decisions affecting occupational futures, commonly made when pupils are aged about fourteen, are whether they are to take courses leading to nationally recognized academic qualifications and, if so, in which subjects they are to take such courses. The first of these decisions, generally made by teachers on the basis of the assessed attainments of pupils, effectively removes from large numbers of young people the possibility of entry to most middle-class occupations. For the remainder, decisions about which subjects to take and which certificates to seek lead to a similar social selection process, but also relate to the type of occupation which pupils later enter. In particular, which pupils will become scientists or technologists is largely determined at this stage.

Preferences among subjects

The attractiveness of different subjects to pupils is a function of the sort of tasks they are asked to undertake in different periods of the timetable. Any one class's experiences of 'history' or 'mathematics' are not likely to be representative. And in view of historical changes in syllabuses and teaching approaches, and of the wide variations which can be found between schools, generalizations about the relative popularity of different subjects are of little value. It is useful, however, to know what makes subjects more or less attractive. Even to achieve this aim necessitates taking large samples of classes to nullify the effect of differences among teachers in the skill with which they carry out similar activities.

One of the most extensive British studies has been that of Pritchard (1935) who asked over eight thousand pupils at forty-seven academic secondary schools to rank subjects in order of popularity and to give reasons for placing subjects first or last. He found that some subjects (e.g. English, history and geography) were assessed largely in terms of whether their *content* was interesting, and that these were generally ranked higher than subjects like mathematics and Latin, which appealed to pupils in so far as the *operations* they involved were found interesting or challenging. The most common reason for disliking this latter group of subjects was pupils' lack of proficiency, a reason rarely given for disliking the content-dominant subjects. Subjects were 'interesting' if they provided variety, gave scope for discussion and argument, dealt with people or were related to everyday life. Another attractive feature of some subjects was the scope they gave for physical activity.

The usefulness of subjects was rarely mentioned by these pupils on academic courses. In a similar study of elementary-school children between the ages of seven and fourteen (Shakespeare, 1936), however, practical utility was found to be more important. Whereas younger pupils' reasons tended to be non-specific or idiosyncratic, achievement became the most common reason for preference around the age of eleven, and reasons of usefulness were dominant among the older pupils. Like Pritchard, Shakespeare found that variety and scope for activity were also important. Practical subjects were most popular with both sexes. Similarly, a more recent study of fifteen-year-old leavers (Morton-Williams and Finch, 1968) found practical and vocational subjects to be distinctive in being generally rated both interesting and useful. In general, these pupils made a clear distinction between subjects that were useful and those which were interesting: for example, less than half of them found mathematics interesting, but over 90 per cent thought it a useful subject.

The conditions of subject choice

At the end of their second or third years in secondary school, many pupils are faced with a choice among several courses. Some of these courses, especially those intended mainly for pupils 'of average ability', are explicitly aimed at specific types of occupation such as clerical work. But although those provided for 'above average' pupils also have occupational implications, what these implications are is not usually clear. Nor is there any single pattern observable over different schools as to the nature of the choice which has to be made.

The set of courses which a school makes available to its pupils at this stage depends on the way in which the headmaster has organized timetables for staff and pupils. Timetabling involves implicit assumptions as to what choices pupils should be free to make. If any group of subjects could be chosen from all those taught in a school, many thousands of different combinations would be possible. But with the conventional type of class-teaching arrangement this would involve many small classes and, therefore, more teachers than are available. The consequent restrictions which are imposed on subject choice vary widely, apparently for two main reasons. The first is that headmasters differ in their preconceptions: 'history or geography, but not both' and 'if biology, then not mathematics' are two of the more common. The second is the variation in the efficiency with which timetables are planned; this is important in affecting the number of possible subject combinations, but also in determining the extent to which unintended incompatibilities between subjects are made apparent and dealt with. McIntosh and Ewan (1970) studied the courses available to 'certificate' pupils in twenty-one Scottish secondary schools. They found that options were presented in two main ways: as a list of complete courses, or as a list of choices, such as the following:

One subject is to be selected from each line:

1. English
2. Arithmetic
3. History/geography
4. Mathematics/home management/biology
5. French/woodwork/metalwork/art/music
6. Latin/history/geography/technical drawing and applied mechanics/home management/dress and design/art/Russian/music
7. Physics and chemistry/biology and chemistry/art/German/music/Greek/commercial subjects/Russian.

In this school it is clear that a large number of different courses are available. Yet German cannot be taken together with science subjects; a general course involving French, Latin, physics and chemistry is incompatible with both art and music; and a course involving mathematics, physics, chemistry and biology is impossible. Some such limitations are inevitable, but often it seems that chance rather than policy determines which subjects shall be incompatible. McIntosh and Ewan found that not only were there general differences between subjects in the number of others with which they were compatible (English, mathematics and geography high; economic organization, German, music and art low), but that the number of other subjects with which some were compatible varied markedly from school to school.

In another study of Scottish secondary schools, Pont and Butcher (1968) found interschool differences of similar magnitude. In the seventeen schools they studied, the number of different courses theoretically available ranged from seven to over a thousand. At one school no general arts–science course was available, whereas at others the options were such that the majority of pupils chose general courses. Of particular interest was the availability of courses including science subjects; the number of different courses of this sort varied between schools from two to 159, and also varied with the sex of pupils. The two extremes were both found in the same school, where all third-year boys, but no third-year girls, did science courses.

Who makes the difficult and important decisions about what course a pupil will follow? Pont and Butcher's findings are consistent with the impressions of others about the general situation. In three schools, they found that the decisions were virtually made by school staff although, in two of these, parents' agreement was sought. The more common procedure was for a list of options to be sent to parents with an invitation to a talk by the headmaster and possibly to a consultation with teachers about their children; alternatively pupils might be individually interviewed or be given a talk about the choice to be made. The option sheet was then left to be completed by parents. In only one of the seventeen schools were there meetings of individual pupils, their parents and their teachers to discuss the choice.

Among factors relevant to these choices are the pupils' interests (probably known best by themselves), their aptitudes (some known best by teachers) and the qualifications necessary for entry to possible occupations or types of higher education (usually known, if by anyone involved, by the headmaster or careers master). With the number of options usually available, rational decision making can only be achieved if priorities are made explicit and a coherent strategy adopted. Information from the school about the choice to be made, like that quoted above, rarely gives much guidance in formulating such strategies or priorities. The adequacy of the decisions, therefore, depends heavily on the knowledge and abilities of parents, their understanding of their children and willingness to consider their preferences, and on their willingness and ability to seek needed information from teachers. There is ample evidence that this last factor is closely related to socio-economic status. Middle-class parents, more career-oriented in their thinking, are more likely to appreciate the importance of this decision, to seek from teachers the information they want and to challenge teachers' opinions or even the school's timetabling arrangements.

Arts or science?

For pupils assessed to be above average in general ability, a dominant feature of the choice they have to make about the age of fourteen is whether to specialize in arts or science subjects. Pont and Butcher (1968) found that, of the pupils in their Scottish sample who took courses which might lead to university entrance, 20 per cent of the boys and over 60 per cent of the girls dropped science at the end of their second year. In England, the choice between arts and science at this stage is, if anything, even more definite. One study of sixth-form boys in seventy-eight grammar and public schools (Oxford University Department of Education, 1963) found that the decision between arts and science had effectively been taken at fourteen by 80 per cent of the sample.

What are the effects of having to make this important career choice at such an early age? In general, career development theory suggests that most adolescents will not by this time have taken account of many factors which would later appear relevant to them, nor will they have crystallized any stable occupational preference. There is evidence, however, that a lasting interest in science tends to be established at an earlier age than an interest in arts; and that those who opt for arts and science courses tend to differ in the reasons behind their choices. Science choices have been found to be more related to occupational intentions and to interests than is the case for non-science specialists, whose choice appears to depend more on their relative attainments in different subjects.

Available evidence does not provide an adequate basis for predicting whether the numbers opting for arts or science subjects would be different if the choice were made later. Especially for girls, however, the nature of the choice presented appears to be an important factor. If, out of the several subject combinations which are made available, only one or two involve science subjects, pupils are more likely to give up science. Brown (1953), for example, found wide variations among girls' grammar schools in the proportions studying science, and concluded that these proportions were determined to a considerable extent by the nature of the alternative courses available.

To what extent do preferences for arts or science subjects result directly from the influence of social environments in which greater emphasis is placed on one or other? Comparisons of the retrospections of students in the two fields have tended to answer this question in the affirmative. Lovell and White (1958) found that among 102 men students in a training college, significantly more of those taking one or more science subjects reported their parents as having had scientific and technical interests and less interest in the arts than did non-science students, and more commonly claimed that their fathers had attempted to stimulate their interest in science. Other such studies have found that reported relationships with specific teachers and the attractiveness with which subjects were said to be presented have been related to choice of specialism. Investigations of current attitudes and environments of adolescents, however, have tended not to substantiate these findings, especially those relating to parental influence. Meyer and Penfold (1961) found that interest in science among pupils in the first and third years of a London school was related neither to parents' interest in science nor to pupils' own attitudes towards their science teachers. Most convincing is the evidence of Butcher (1969a) who categorized Scottish second-year pupils on the basis of a large number of attainment, personality and interest measures as being particularly suited to science or arts courses or as equally likely to specialize in either. Taking a stratified sample of pupils in terms of this classification, he correlated pupil variables with a wide variety of parent variables, assessed by interviews, which might be relevant to arts–science preference. Correlations between parent and child variables were generally low and provided no evidence to support the hypothesis that parental interests are 'inherited'. Butcher has found, however, that the courses actually chosen are often not those which would be predicted; so it may be that the tendency for retrospective and concurrent studies to give different results is explicable on the grounds that the former have generally been concerned with choices and the latter mainly with interests and preferences.

Earlier in this chapter it was seen that career choice in general may be conceived as a process whereby people with certain personal characteristics tend to be drawn towards certain careers; or, perhaps more adequately, as a process in which individuals relate their beliefs about themselves to their beliefs about different careers. Both approaches are relevant to the specific choice which adolescents have to make between arts and science specialisms.

There is a wealth of evidence that physical scientists tend to have distinctive interests, values and personalities; for example, scientists have generally been found to gain greater satisfaction from complex intellectual activities and less from social intercourse than do most other occupational groups. Are such distinctive patterns apparent when the important curricular choice has to be made in early adolescence? Butcher (1969b), from a factor analysis of measures of attainment, personality, interests and attitudes towards teachers, subjects and careers for his sample of a thousand Scottish thirteen year olds, extracted ten clearly interpretable oblique (not completely independent) factors. Of these, six indicated different subject–career orientations – scientific, mechanical, mathematical-computational, literary, social work, and aesthetic. Interesting features of the loading patterns on these variables include the general tendencies for interest and preference variables to have the highest loadings, for attainment loadings to be substantial and for loadings on personality variables to be negligible (except for a close relationship between mechanical orientation and toughmindedness). Another possibly significant feature is that, while all the high loadings for the scientific factor indicate positive enthusiasm or aptitude, all other orientation factors have sizeable negative loadings, suggesting that orientation towards one field involves a definite rejection of others.

Although showing that clear patterns of preference do appear to be established by the age of thirteen, Butcher's evidence suggests that personality differences are not very relevant except in so far as they are reflected in differential attainments. Work in recent years, notably that of Hudson (1966), has indicated that such a relation between abilities and personality may be important in subject choice. Studying pupils in the sixth forms of independent boys' schools, Hudson found that subject specialization was closely related to pupils' relative abilities for divergent thinking (fluency in the production of unusual and interesting ideas) and convergent thinking (the type of ability assessed in most intelligence tests). Those specializing in mathematics or the physical sciences tended to perform much better on intelligence tests than on tests such as 'How many uses can you think of for each of the following objects?'; and the reverse was true for specialists in history, modern languages and English literature. Further exploratory studies have suggested that such biases are observable among younger pupils, and that those whose bias is towards convergent thinking tend to be relatively conventional in their thinking, less likely to express feelings of violence or infantile impulses or to be interested in people, to be more conformist and influenced by established authority, and to be more bound in their academic studies by the demands of the school syllabus.

Other studies have broadly supported Hudson's central finding, although several qualifications must be made: the low reliability of tests of divergent thinking means that results must be viewed with caution, especially in view of the smallness of the samples which have generally been used; several different divergent-thinking abilities may be distinguished, as distinct from one another as any are from (convergent) general intelligence; and the relationship between cognitive bias and arts/science choice appears to vary considerably with the social and educational context.

Since successful original work in any field of academic study, and especially in science, requires both convergent and divergent thinking, it is not self-evident that an individual's cognitive bias should predispose him to choose one specialism rather than another. That such bias none the less appears highly relevant to sixth formers has been shown by an analysis of answers to an A-level General Studies Paper question asking for explanations of the current relative 'swing from science' (Ashton and Meredith, 1969). The two reasons most commonly given were the high level of intelligence seen as necessary for the study of natural sciences, and the lack of scope they seem to give for self-expression.

The search for an explanation of this connection leads one to a consideration of adolescents' occupational and self-concepts. Within Western societies, there are fairly elaborate stereotypes of artists and scientists which are widely shared. On the basis of evidence from several small samples, Hudson (1968) concluded that these stereotypes are accepted equally by pupils specializing in arts and science, and that they have been learned by the age of entry to secondary school. Mathematicians, physicists and engineers were, he found, perceived as dependable, intelligent, cold and unsociable, while poets, artists and novelists were thought of as warm, exciting, sociable and imaginative. Whereas scientists were considered most 'valuable', artists were generally judged to be more attractive. Fifteen year olds, asked to rate their actual, ideal, perceived (by teachers) and future selves on several scales, manifested self-concepts which corresponded to their specialism. With regard to 'artistic virtues' the two groups differed most in their ratings of actual self, and with regard to 'scientific virtues' they differed most in their ratings of perceived self; this indicates, Hudson suggested, the importance of attitudes to external authority in differentiating the two groups. Also significant is his finding that divergers showed the greatest differences among their four self-concepts, and particularly between their actual and future selves; divergers appear to be unwilling to commit themselves during ado-lescence to being a certain type of person (and therefore to choosing a certain type of occupation) in the future.

Hudson found pupils in the early stages of secondary school unable to express differentiated self-concepts, thus leaving open the question of whether the relation of self-concepts to occupational stereotypes affects the initial choice of specialism. But other evidence suggests that the majority of boys in early adolescence perceive scientific careers as highly attractive. Butcher and Pont (1968), for example, found that when 150 able thirteen year olds ranked fifteen occupations on criteria of preference, inter-est, salaries, prestige, qualifications required and usefulness to society, science careers were ranked among the highest on all criteria; the six careers requiring scientific qualifica-tions were among the seven most preferred. For a com-parable sample of girls, however, scientific careers were generally perceived as uninteresting, and only that of medi-cal doctor was among the six most preferred, although on the other four criteria girls' rankings were very similar to those of boys.

Of the many unanswered questions with regard to arts-science choice, the causes of this early aversion to scientific studies on the part of the great majority of girls is perhaps the most obvious. It is clear that cultural preconceptions about the roles appropriate for the two sexes are of major importance; but we do not know the precise nature of these preconceptions in relation to science, how they are ex-pressed in the behaviour of parents and teachers, or how they affect the development of girls' interests.

In considering the choices which pupils make between arts and science, some attention must be given to the dis-tinctive position of mathematics. Apart from a tradition in many schools of offering biology and mathematics as alternative subjects, science courses almost always include mathematics; and qualifications in mathematics are necess-ary for the great majority of scientific careers. Yet the attractions which science and mathematics hold for adolescents can be very different, as Butcher's (1969b) study has demonstrated. On the mathematical-computational factor which he extracted, the highest loading was for pupils' ratings of mathematics as a school subject; but this factor was quite independent of the scientific orientation factor, on which the loading for liking of mathematics was only 0·18 and that for mathematics marks only 0·11. Whereas science subjects such as chemistry tend to be attractive because of interest in the phenomena examined and the pleasures of exploration and discovery, the attractions of mathematics are largely in the intellectual challenge it presents and in the satisfaction which it can give of 'being correct'. Interest and attainment in mathematics have generally been found to be more closely related than is the case for other school subjects; and much the most common reason given for disliking mathematics is lack of success in the subject.

Hudson (1968), in his investigation of adolescents' stereotypes of different occupational groups, found that the mathematician was the least attractive figure of all those presented, and that this figure embodied to an extreme degree those characteristics of intelligence, dependability, coldness and unimaginativeness which were generally associated with scientists. Among the different scientific figures presented, these characteristics were associated most with the physicist, whose work may be seen as more mathematical and abstract than that of the engineer or biologist. One might, therefore, hypothesize that, while the attractions of mathematics and science are different, a dominant reason for disliking science is that it involves mathematics or activities seen to be similar to mathematics.

Science and technology

After the usual initial decision by the age of fourteen to specialize in arts or science subjects, pupils wishing to go on to higher education generally have to make further decisions about subjects in which to specialize. Many of these later decisions are consciously career-oriented, but little is known about the factors affecting them. Information which would be valuable would include evidence about the extent to which the range of sixth-form courses available limits choice, about the adequacy of the information received by pupils about university entrance requirements and the extent to which these requirements affect the subject combinations chosen for sixth-form study, and about factors affecting the choice of higher education courses by those pupils who have not by this stage crystallized clear occupational preferences.

A distinction can be made between those courses of higher education aimed at preparing students for particular occupations, such as teaching, medicine or agriculture, and those which do not imply any such occupational commitment. For students who have taken science courses at school, a choice which tends to be related to this distinction is between courses in pure and applied science. In a study, conducted by the Oxford University Department of Education (1963), of over 1400 boys taking sixth-form science courses in England and Wales, it was found that three-quarters of those taking pure-science courses had not decided on a definite occupation; these courses, unlike those in engineering, were thought to allow students to retain their freedom of choice.

Studies of the personal characteristics of engineers and scientists have repeatedly found that engineers tend to be more sociable, to find more pleasure in working out of doors and with their hands, to be less interested in ideas, and to be more toughminded and concerned about material and financial aspects of their work than are pure scientists. These differences are reflected in the images which pupils in the Oxford study had of pure and applied scientists and in the reasons they gave for favouring one or other. While choices appear to be delayed until the sixth form, Butcher (1969b) has found that such orientations towards pure and applied science can be clearly distinguished among thirteen year olds. His scientific- and mechanical-orientation factors, although having a correlation of 0·36 between them and having in common sizeable loadings on measures of liking for science, are differentiated by the relative prominence on the latter of loadings for mechanical and outdoor interests and for the career of engineering, by the definite rejection it involves of social service and clerical careers, and by its association with toughmindedness.

Several investigators have found engineering to be the most popular of all careers among British adolescent boys of high ability. But among those of the Oxford sample who went on to higher education courses, those specializing in pure science tended to have the best A-level results, followed in order by university students of engineering, medical students, and students taking Diploma in Technology courses. Evidence from North America and European countries, however, suggests that the tendency for the ablest students to prefer pure science to engineering and technology is considerably greater in England than elsewhere. One probable reason for this is the low status accorded to technologists in this country, especially in academic circles. In the group of sixth formers cited above there was general agreement that engineering ranked very low amongst graduate occupations in the intelligence it required, in the income it gave and, especially, in prestige. And pupils learn to think of engineering in these terms at an early age: among the Scottish thirteen year olds studied by Butcher and Pont (1968), engineering was rated the most attractive of fifteen careers, but on salary, prestige and qualifications required it ranked below all other scientific careers except science teaching.

The academic ethos of grammar schools may contribute to this tendency for the most able pupils to decide against a technological career. Hume (1968) found significantly different trends with age in attitudes towards engineering as a career in a grammar school and a technical school: in the latter, boys in their fourth year had more favourable attitudes than those in their second year, while in the former the opposite was the case. There are many possible explanations for this difference, but differences in the value placed upon working with one's hands and in the opportunities given to do this in the two types of school may be hypothesized as likely contributory factors. Furthermore, grammar-school science curricula, which tend to emphasize the *explanation* much more than the *control* of natural phenomena, may contribute to the glamorous notions of 'pure' research which many sixth formers in the Oxford study were found to share; a widespread belief among them was that, whereas such research requires intelligence and presents challenging problems with the possibility of exciting discoveries, applied research and development rarely involve more than the routine application of what is already understood. This investigation also revealed a second way in which grammar-school curricula may influence pupils away from technological careers. About 40 per cent of pupils reported that having chosen their school subjects without any career in mind, they then chose careers to suit A-level qualifications they expected to obtain. As might be expected, this basis for choosing careers and higher education courses was more common among those continuing with the study of pure science than among those taking up the new studies involved in engineering courses.

Schools and occupational guidance

In addition to influencing the subject preferences of pupils and the types of educational qualifications they obtain, schools may influence occupational choices more directly. The majority of adolescents make their initial choice of occupation while they are at school, and information and guidance given by teachers or others in the school may, therefore, play an important part in the decision-making process.

This influence can be exerted through questions relevant to occupations arising in the course of ordinary classwork, through informal discussions between teachers and individual pupils, or through a formal system for careers information and advice arranged by headmasters or careers teachers. The school also provides the context in which

Youth Employment Officers first meet and advise pupils. And the curriculum may be deliberately organized in order to give pupils information about, or even experience of, a variety of occupations. (Such curricular arrangements, approved by the *Newsom Report*, 1963, are to be distinguished from those courses, also recommended by that Report, which are planned around a supposed centre of interest in a specific occupation; the latter, rather than providing information and experience which might help pupils to make a choice, are based on the assumption that many fourteen-year-old pupils already have stable occupational preferences, and the courses concentrate on preparing them for these preferred occupations.)

The nature of the occupational guidance which it is relevant for schools to give varies according to the age at which pupils leave school, their academic qualifications and, therefore, the level of the occupations between which they are likely to choose. The older pupils are when they leave school, the more career-oriented, self-aware and accustomed to abstract thinking they are likely to be; and the higher the level of the occupations which are open to them, the more clearly prescribed, in general, will be the qualifications and training necessary for entry to these occupations. In view of these factors, and also of the concentration of career development research on higher-level occupations, the needs and demands of older leavers are most likely to be for specifiable information which schools should generally be able to provide. For early leavers, on the other hand, precise information is less likely to be either sought or available, except in terms of specific jobs which are locally available. Because many of these pupils and their parents expect to choose not careers but jobs, and because they are starting work before reaching an age at which they are likely to have formulated any clear occupational self-concepts, there is room for considerable disagreement about the nature of the guidance which it is most appropriate for schools to give. Obvious goals, however, include extending pupils' awareness of the various considerations which may be relevant in occupational choice, and helping them to achieve a clearer conception of the various duties involved, satisfactions to be gained and frustrations to be borne in as wide as possible a range of occupations, including some immediately available and some dependent on further education.

Evidence of the occupationally relevant expectations which pupils and their parents have of schools is available from a national inquiry carried out for the Schools Council (Morton-Williams and Finch, 1968). Within a random stratified sample of almost five thousand pupils between the ages of thirteen and sixteen in England and Wales, the inquiry concentrated on those who intended to leave school, or who had left, at fifteen. The great majority of these pupils and their parents rated as very important objectives of secondary education that pupils' attainments should help them to get good jobs, and that what was learned at school should be of direct use in their jobs. In addition, the school's tasks in facilitating decision making by teaching about different sorts of jobs and in preparing pupils for the realities of work were rated very important by 74 per cent and 60 per cent of the pupils respectively. Over half the pupils wanted advice from the school or Youth Employment Officer about the type of work to which they would be suited, and two-thirds wanted help in finding a job. In each respect, parents tended to want more help for their children than did the pupils themselves, and over 60 per cent of parents would themselves have liked more information about types of jobs available and about their children's abilities.

Teachers in schools where there was a sizeable number of fifteen-year-old leavers, and especially the headmasters of these schools, gave much less emphasis than parents or pupils to career-related attainments and attached rather less importance to informing pupils about occupations or preparing them for work. None the less, although almost all headmasters reported that staff members were already engaged in giving information and advice on careers and in preparing pupils for their first experience of work, about half of them, and a larger proportion of careers teachers, thought that more should be done in each of these respects. Thus, although not matching pupils' or parents' concern about occupations, many schools appear to desire an improvement upon existing arrangements; and this is reflected in the increase in recent years in the number of schools with teachers who have some training in careers guidance and who are given time for this work. Since most of the investigations reported below were carried out some years ago, it is possible that their results underestimate the present influence of schools on occupational choice.

School influence on occupational choice

Objective differentiation of school from other influences on occupational choice would require, at the very least, the same types of large-scale survey using multivariate statistical techniques as have been used in attempts to identify factors affecting school attainments; and the use of such techniques would depend upon the precise specification of key criterion variables in the process of occupational choice. In the absence of any such studies, one is dependent on people's subjective reports of who and what have influenced them in their choices, and on comparisons between descriptions of the choice behaviour manifested by adolescents and the prescriptions made by teachers of the sort of choice behaviour which is desirable: the greater the discrepancy, the less, one must assume, is the influence of the school.

Investigations carried out in various parts of Britain during the last twenty years, of the ways in which pupils in secondary-modern schools choose their occupations, have obtained fairly consistent results. While intensely held occupational ambitions are unusual, the majority of pupils have established fairly stable preferences by their final year at school. Such stability of preference does not, however, generally result from any systematic consideration of alternatives. Choices are often determined by chance factors, such as the occupations of aunts and uncles, or the casual comments of friends about their own jobs; Carter (1962, p. 111) quoted as fairly typical the way in which one girl's choice was made: 'Me and my mother were out shopping one day and passed a wallpaper shop, and there was a girl, ever so busy, selling it. Mum said "You'd be alright in a wallpaper shop"', and that was that. Most research supports Jahoda's (1952) conclusion that choices are largely based on the combined effects of three types of experience: direct personal experience, for example with hobbies and with school subjects; the reported experiences of friends and relations; and the general climate of opinion in the social groups to which adolescents belong which may emphasize, for example, the importance for boys of learning a trade or the undesirability of factory work for girls.

Knowledge of the types of job locally available, and even of the tasks involved in jobs which are pupils' first choices, has typically been found to be very small. In general, school-leavers appear to be unable to think of more than three or four different jobs available to them, and even these jobs are most commonly described in such general terms as 'steelworks', 'shops', or by the names of firms. The proportion of pupils who have a reasonable idea of the nature of the work they have chosen has been estimated at one-third or less and as many as 40 per cent have been found to know no more than the name of the chosen job. This ignorance is paralleled by a lack of ideas about what considerations might be relevant in selecting jobs. Carter (1962), for example, reported that 'a substantial number' couldn't say why they wanted to do the work which they aimed at. Jahoda and Chalmers (1963) found that, in a sample of leavers from Scottish junior-secondary schools, the average number of criteria mentioned as relevant, other than pay, was less than two; and they describe these pupils' ideas about how to choose a job as 'poverty-stricken'.

Little detailed evidence is available about what influence teachers attempt to exert on the job-choosing behaviour of leavers, but it would be surprising if many were satisfied with findings like those described above. Carter found that teachers tended to emphasize the importance of thinking about what jobs to aim at, of viewing one's first job as the start of a career, and of selecting jobs because of their intrinsic attractiveness rather than because of wages and conditions. Much of this advice, he found, was dismissed as irrelevant preaching; often it was too general for pupils to be able to relate it to their own particular problems; and, since advice was generally given in occasional remarks rather than in a context of systematic explanation and discussion, it was usually forgotten.

From pupils' own reports, as well as from their behaviour, it appears that the influence of teachers is very slight; Jahoda (1952), for example, found it to be 'negligible'. Although parents can exert a dominant influence, many give very little guidance and the majority leave their children a great deal of freedom in choosing jobs; it is not the advice of teachers, however, but that of relatives or friends, which is commonly mentioned as supplementing that given by parents. This position may have been modified in recent years by the increased importance given to careers work in many schools, but wherever advice from teachers to early leavers conflicts with that received in the home environment, it is the latter which is likely to prevail. Since few working-class parents have either the information or the experience with which to help their children choose a career, and since the majority of parents would welcome information and advice in this area, there seems good reason to believe that schools are most likely to influence career choice where they establish effective communication with parents.

Teachers in grammar schools tend to exert much more influence on career choice than do those in secondary-modern schools. Chown (1958) found, for a sample of grammar-school pupils mostly aged fifteen or sixteen, that slightly more than half had received help from school staff in the choice of occupations, whereas only about a quarter of the sample reported that their parents had made a positive contribution. The great importance of staff, she concluded, 'is not that they provide original ideas, but that they help in assessing the suitability of ideas gleaned from other sources'. It may be that the way in which Chown's questions were worded makes the influence of teachers, in comparison with that of parents, seem greater than it is. In another English study (Hill, 1965), sixth-form boys, asked which adults had helped most in the choice of careers, named parents three times as often as school staff; even this result, however, suggests that grammar-school teachers exert considerable influence. These boys, from maintained grammar schools in the Midlands, mentioned teachers four times as often as headmasters, and subject and careers teachers approximately equally often.

The Youth Employment Service

Statutory provision for occupational guidance in the United Kingdom is made through the Youth Employment Service. For most school-leavers, however, the guidance which the YES is able to offer is limited to what can be done through one group talk and one short individual interview during the last year at school. Partly because of this, perhaps, it is widely viewed as merely a job-finding agency. Jahoda and Chalmers (1963) found that 84 per cent of their sample thought, before their interviews, that this was the function of the Youth Employment Officer, and 63 per cent still thought so afterwards; yet this was in an area where the Service was thought to be better than average.

The 'effectiveness' of the talks must vary widely according to the audience, the adequacy of the preparation which the school has given them for it, the competence of the YEO, and the goals which he sets himself. Quite a large minority of pupils, especially in secondary-modern schools, appear to be encouraged by the talks to think systematically about jobs, often for the first time. Jahoda (1952) found that a few pupils changed their choices as a result of the talk, and that for larger numbers it was influential either in crystallizing tentative ideas or in raising doubts about choices which had previously been unquestioned. There are, however, inevitable limitations to what can be achieved by a single talk. One of the problems is that it has to be sufficiently near the time when pupils intend to leave school for the YEO to be able to assume some concern on their part about the jobs they are going to do; yet by this time large numbers of the pupils have decided what jobs they want, and to them the relevant questions are not about choosing jobs but about finding them. The interview also is limited in its value by the shortage of time available, and by most pupils' lack of understanding of its purpose. To the great majority it is seen as an occasion on which to inform the YEO of desired jobs in order that he can help with placement. Questions asked about anything other than occupational preferences, therefore, tend to be considered irrelevant. Accordingly, the most common criticisms made by pupils, especially by early leavers, is that discussions at the interviews are too general and vague (Morton-Williams and Finch, 1968). Other common criticisms are, from those who already have jobs 'fixed up', that there was no point to the interview and, from others, that the YEO attempted to persuade them to change decisions they had already made. While about 50 per cent of pupils appear to consider the interview helpful in some way, few modify their job aims as a result of it. This lack of change is partly because the majority of recommendations made by YEOs are consistent with the stated preferences of pupils, although sometimes clarifying these preferences. In view of the inadequacy of the information and thought on which most preferences are based, this degree of agreement would be surprising if conditions allowed YEOs to do anything but detect the most inappropriate of choices.

As Carter (1962), for example, has shown, the Youth Employment Service can be even less effective in another of its duties, that of following up pupils in their first years of employment. Over half of those in his sample did not initially enter the occupations they wanted, over a third changed jobs during their first year of work and many others were discontented with their jobs; yet the guidance function of the Service, as opposed to that of finding jobs, appeared to be effectively over for these adolescents when they took their first jobs. It seems clear that the Youth Employment Service, although giving the majority of pupils more help than they receive from their teachers, does not have the facilities and staffing which would allow it adequately to carry out its function.

If the task of helping young people to choose occupations and careers which they will find satisfying is to be taken seriously, much more intensive programmes of education and guidance, spread over several years, are needed. This will require members of school staffs who have specialist knowledge of career development and decision making and who are trained in the skills of counselling. It is only now that such people are becoming available for the first time in Britain; it remains to be seen what roles they will be allotted in British schools and the effectiveness with which they will be able to fulfil these roles.

References

ABRAMSON, P. (1967), 'The differential political socialization of English secondary school students', *Sociol. Educ.* vol. 40, pp. 246–69.

ADELSON, J., and O'NEIL, R. (1966), 'The growth of political ideas in adolescence: the sense of community', *J. Personal. soc. Psychol.*, vol. 4, pp. 295–306.

ADORNO, T. W., FRENKEL-BRUNSWIK, E., LEVINSON, D. J., and SANFORD, R. N. (1950), *The Authoritarian Personality*, Harper & Row.

ALLPORT, G. W. (1954), *The Nature of Prejudice*, Addison-Wesley.

ALMOND, G., and VERBA, S. (1963), *The Civic Culture*, Princeton University Press.

ALVES, C. (1968), *Religion and the Secondary School*, SCM Press.

ARGYLE, M. (1969), *Social Interaction*, Methuen.

ARGYLE, M., and ROBINSON, P. (1962), 'Two origins of achievement motivation', *Brit. J. soc. clin. Psychol.*, vol. 1, pp. 107–20.

ARONFREED, J., (1961), 'The nature, variety, and social patterning of moral responses to transgression', *J. abnorm, soc. Psychol.*, vol. 62, pp. 223–41.

ASCH, S. E. (1946), 'Forming impressions of personality', *J. abnorm. soc. Psychol.*, vol. 41, pp. 258–90.

ASHBY, B., MORRISON, A., and BUTCHER, H. J. (1970), 'The abilities and attainments of immigrant children', *Res. Educ.*, vol. 4, pp. 73–80.

ASHTON, B. G., and MEREDITH, H. M. (1969), 'Attitudes to science and scientists: the attitudes of sixth-formers', *School Sci. Rev.*, vol. 51, pp. 15–19.

ATKINSON, J. W. (1957), 'Motivational determinants of risk-taking behavior', *Psychol. Rev.*, vol. 64, pp. 359–72.

AUSUBEL, D. P., and AUSUBEL, P. (1963), 'Ego development among segregated Negro children', in A. H. Passow (ed.), *Education in Depressed Areas*, Teachers College, Columbia University.

BANDURA, A., and MCDONALD, F. J. (1963), 'Influence of social reinforcement and the behavior of models in shaping children's moral judgements', *J. abnorm. soc. Psychol.*, vol. 67, pp. 274–81.

BANDURA, A., and WALTERS, R. H. (1959), *Adolescent Aggression*, Ronald Press.

BANDURA, A., ROSS, D., and ROSS, S. (1963), 'A comparative test of the status, envy, social power, and the secondary reinforcement theories of identificatory learning', *J. abnorm. soc. Psychol.*, vol. 67, pp. 527–34.

BARATZ, S. S., and BARATZ, J. C. (1970), 'Early childhood intervention: the social science base of institutional racism', *Harv. educ. Rev.*, vol. 40, pp. 29–50.

BARKER LUNN, J. C. (1970), *Streaming in the Primary School*, National Foundation for Educational Research in England and Wales.

BARR, F. (1959), 'Urban and rural differences in ability and attainment', *Educ. Res.*, vol. 1, pp. 49–60.

BEREITER, C., and ENGELMANN, S. (1966), *Teaching Disadvantaged Children in the Preschool*, Prentice-Hall.

BERENDA, R. W. (1940), *The Influence of the Group on the Judgements of Children*, Columbia University Press.

BERNSTEIN, B. (1961), 'Social class and linguistic development: a theory of social learning', in A. H. Halsey, J. Floud and C. A. Anderson (eds.), *Education, Economy and Society*, Free Press, pp. 288–314.

BERNSTEIN, B. (1965), 'A socio-linguistic approach to social learning', in J. Gould (ed.), *Penguin Survey of the Social Sciences 1965*, Penguin, pp. 145–66.

BERNSTEIN, B. (1970), 'A critique of the concept of "compensatory education"', in D. Rubinstein and C. Stoneman (eds.), *Education for Democracy*, Penguin, pp. 110–21.

BOARDMAN, R. (1969), 'The theory and practice of educational simulation', *Educ. Res.*, vol. 11, pp. 179–84.

BROADBENT, D. E, (1964), *Behaviour*, Methuen.

BROWN, N. M. (1953), 'Some educational influences on the choice of a science career by grammar school girls', *Brit. J. educ. Psychol.*, vol. 23, pp. 188–95.

BRUCKMANN, I. R. (1966), 'The relationship between achievement motivation and sex, age, social class, school stream and intelligence', *Brit. J. soc. clin. Psychol.*, vol. 5, pp. 211–20.

BUELL, J., STODDARD, P., HARRIS, R., and BAER, D. (1968), 'Collateral social development accompanying reinforcement of outdoor play in a pre-school child', *J. appl. behav. Anal.*, vol. 1, pp. 167–73.

BURTON, R. V. (1963), 'The generality of honesty reconsidered', *Psychol. Rev.*, vol. 70, pp. 481–500.

BUTCHER, H. J. (1968), *Human Intelligence: Its Nature and Assessment*, Methuen.

BUTCHER, H. J. (1969a), 'An investigation of the "swing from science"', *Res. Educ.*, vol. 1, pp. 38–57.

BUTCHER, H. J. (1969b), 'The structure of abilities, interests and personality in 1,000 Scottish schoolchildren', *Brit. J. educ. Psychol.*, vol. 39, pp. 154–65.

BUTCHER, H. J., and PONT, H. B. (1968), 'Opinions about careers among Scottish secondary school children of high ability', *Brit. J. educ. Psychol.*, vol. 38, pp. 272–9.

CAMPBELL, J. D., and YARROW, M. R. (1958), 'Personal and situational variables in adaptation to change', *J. soc. Iss.*, vol. 14, pp. 29–46.

CARTER, M. P. (1962), *Home, School and Work*, Pergamon.

CENTERS, R. (1963), 'A laboratory adaptation of the conversational procedure for the conditioning of verbal operants', *J. abnorm. soc. Psychol.*, vol. 67, pp. 334–9.

CENTRAL ADVISORY COUNCIL FOR EDUCATION (ENGLAND) (1954), *Early Leaving*, HMSO.

CHERRYHOLMES, C. H. (1966), 'Some current research on effectiveness of educational simulations: implications for alternative strategies', *Amer. behav. Sci.*, vol. 10, p. 4.

CHILD, I. L., STORM, T., and VEROFF, J. (1958), 'Achievement themes in folk-tales related to socialization practice', in J. W. Atkinson (ed.), *Motives in Fantasy, Action and Society*, Van Nostrand, pp. 479–92.

CHOWN, S. M. (1958), 'The formation of occupational choice among grammar school pupils', *Occup. Psychol.*, vol. 32, pp. 171–82.

CHRISTIANSEN, B. (1959), *Attitudes towards Foreign Affairs as a Function of Personality*, Oslo University Press.

CHRISTIE, R, (1954), 'Authoritarianism re-examined', in R. Christie and M. Jahoda (eds.), *Studies in the Scope and Method of 'The Authoritarian Personality'*, Free Press.

CICIRELLI, V. G., *et al.* (1969), *The Impact of Head Start: An Evaluation of the Effects of Head Start on Children's Cognitive and Affective Development*, Office of Economic Opportunity, Washington, DC.

COLEMAN, J. S. (1960), 'The adolescent subculture and academic achievement', *Amer. J. Soc.*, vol. 65, pp. 337–47.

COLEMAN, J. S. (ed.) (1965), *Education and Political Development*, Princeton University Press.

COLEMAN, J. S., *et al.* (1966), *Equality of Educational Opportunity*, US Office of Education Report, National Center for Educational Statistics, Washington, DC.

CONVERSE, P. E. (1964), 'The nature of belief systems in mass publics', in D. Apter (ed.), *Ideology and Discontent*, Free Press.

COOPER, B., MAPES, R., and McQUAIL, D. (1966), 'An assessment of a schools television series', *Educ. Rev.*, vol. 19, pp. 33–44.

COOPER, P. (1965), 'The development of the concept of war', *J. Peace Res.*, vol. 1, pp. 1–17.

COOPERSMITH, S. (1967), *The Antecedents of Self-Esteem*, W. H. Freeman.

CRISWELL, J. H. (1939), 'A sociometric study of race cleavage in the classroom', *Arch. Psychol.*, vol. 33, no. 235.

CURRIE, K. (1962), 'A study of the English comprehensive school, with particular reference to the educational, social and cultural effects of the single-sex and co-educational types of school', Ph.D. thesis, University of London.

DALE, R. R. (1968), 'Co-education', in H. J. Butcher (ed.), *Educational Research in Britain*, University of London Press, pp. 243–60.

DAVE, R. H. (1963), 'The identification and measurement of environmental process variables that are related to educational achievement', doctoral dissertation, University of Chicago. (Summarized by B. S. Bloom, A. Davis and R. Hess in *Compensatory Education for Cultural Deprivation*, Holt, Rinehart & Winston, 1965.)

DAVIS, A. (1948), *Social Class Influences upon Learning. Inglis Lecture*, Harvard University Press.

DAVIS, F., and OLESON, V. L. (1965), 'The career outlook of professionally educated women', *Psychiatry*, vol. 28, pp. 334–45.

DOUGLAS, J. W. B. (1964), *The Home and The School*, MacGibbon & Kee.

DOUGLAS, J. W. B., ROSS, J. M., and SIMPSON, H. R. (1968), *All Our Future*, Peter Davies.

EASTON, D., and DENNIS, J. (1967), 'The child's acquisition of regime norms: political efficacy', *Amer. polit. Sci. Rev.*, vol. 61, pp. 25–38.

EGGLESTONE, S. J. (1965), 'Staying-on in non-selective secondary schools', M.A. thesis, University of London.

ENTWISTLE, N. J. (1968), 'Academic motivation and school attainment', *Brit. J. educ. Psychol.*, vol. 38, pp. 181–8.

EYSENCK, H. J. (1954), *The Psychology of Politics*, Routledge & Kegan Paul.

EYSENCK, H. J. (1960), 'The development of moral values in children: the contribution of learning theory', *Brit. J. educ. Psychol.*, vol. 30, pp. 11–12.

FEINBERG, M. R. (1953), 'Relations of background experience to social acceptance', *J. abnorm. soc. Psychol.*, vol. 48, pp. 206–214.

FLOUD, J. S., HALSEY, A. H., and MARTIN, F. M. (1957), *Social Class and Educational Opportunity*, Heinemann.

FRASER, E. D. (1959), *Home Environment and the School*, University of London Press.

FRENKEL-BRUNSWIK, E. (1948), 'A study of prejudice in children', *Hum. Rel.*, vol. 1, pp. 295–306.

FREUD, S. (1923), *The Ego and the Id*, Hogarth Press, 1950.

FREUD, S. (1932), *New Introductory Lectures in Psycho-Analysis*, Norton.

GELATT, H. B. (1962), 'Decision making: a conceptual frame of reference for counselling', *J. counsel. Psychol.*, vol. 9, pp. 240–45.

GINZBERG, E., GINSBURG, S. W., AXELROD, S., and HERMA, J. L. (1951), *Occupational Choice: An Approach to a General Theory*, Columbia University Press.

GLUECK, S., and GLUECK, E. T. (1950), *Unraveling Juvenile Delinquency*, Commonwealth Fund, New York.

GOLDBERG, A. L. (1956), 'The effects of two types of sound motion pictures on the attitudes of adults towards minorities', *J. educ. Sociol.*, vol. 29, pp 386–91.

GOLDBERG, M. L., PASSOW, A. H., and JUSTMAN, J. (1966), *The Effects of Ability Grouping*, Teachers College Press.

GOLDMAN, R. J., and TAYLOR, F. M. (1966), 'Coloured immigrant children: a survey of research studies and literature on their educational problems and potential – (1) in Britain', *Educ. Res.*, vol. 8, pp. 163–83.

GOLDSEN, R. K., ROSENBERG, M., WILLIAMS, R. J., and SUCHMAN, E. (1960), *What College Students Think*, Van Nostrand.

GRANT, N. (1964), *Soviet Education*, Penguin.

GREENSTEIN, F. (1965), *Children and Politics*, Yale University Press.

GREENSTEIN, F. (1969), 'Queen and Prime Minister – the child's eye view', *New Soc.*, vol. 14, no. 369, pp. 635–8.

GROSS, N., and HERRIOTT, R. E. (1965), *Staff Leadership in Public Schools*, Wiley.

GUSKIN, A. E., and GUSKIN, S. L. (1970), *A Social Psychology of Education*, Addison-Wesley.

HAGEN, D. (1960), 'Careers and family atmosphere: a test of Roe's theory', *J. counsel. Psychol.*, vol. 7, pp. 251–6.

HALLAM, R. N. (1967), Logical thinking in history', *Educ. Rev.*, vol. 19, pp.183–202.

HARGREAVES, D. H. (1967), *Social Relations in a Secondary School*, Routledge & Kegan Paul.

HARTLEY, E. L., ROSENBAUM, M., and SCHWARTZ, S. (1948), 'Children's use of ethnic frames of reference', *J. Psychol.*, vol. 26, pp. 367–86.

HARTSHORNE, H., and MAY, M. A. (1928–30), *Studies in the Nature of Character*, Macmillan Co.

HAYES, M. L., and CONKLIN, M. E. (1953), 'Intergroup attitudes and experimental change', *J. exp. Educ.*, vol. 22, pp. 19–36.

HEBRON, M. E., and RIDLEY, F. (1965), 'Characteristics associated with racial prejudice in adolescent boys', *Brit. J. soc. clin. Psychol.*, vol. 4, pp. 92–7.

HERRIOTT, R. E. (1963), 'Some social determinants of educational aspirations', *Harv. educ. Rev.*, vol. 33, pp. 157–77.

HERRIOTT, R. E., and ST JOHN, N. H. (1966), *Social Class and the Urban School*, Wiley.

HERSHENSON, D. B., and ROTH, R. M. (1966), 'A decisional process model of vocational development', *J. counsel. Psychol.*, vol. 13, pp. 368–70.

HESS, R. D., and EASTON, D. (1960), 'The child's image of the President', *Pub. Opin. Quart.*, vol. 24, pp. 632–44.

HESS, R. D., and TORNEY, J. V. (1967), *The Development of Political Attitudes in Children*, Aldine.

HICKS, D. J. (1965), 'Imitation and retention of film-mediated aggressive peer and adult models', *J. Personal. soc. Psychol.*, vol. 2, pp. 97–100.

HILL, G. B. (1965), 'Choice of career by grammar school boys', *Occup. Psychol.*, vol. 39, pp. 279–87.

HILTON, T. L. (1962), 'Career decision-making', *J. counsel. Psychol.*, vol. 9, pp. 291–8.

HIMMELWEIT, H., OPPENHEIM, A. N., and VINCE, P. (1958), *Television and the Child*, Oxford University Press.

HIND, A. G. (1964), 'The comprehensive school with special reference to the house system', Dip. Ed. thesis, University of Nottingham Institute of Education.

HOFFMAN, L., and HOFFMAN, M. (eds.) (1966), *Review of Child Development Research*, Russell Sage Foundation, New York.

HOFFMAN, M. (1963), 'Early processes in moral development', paper read at the Social Science Research Council Conference on Character Development, New York, November.

HOLLAND, J. L. (1966), *The Psychology of Vocational Choice*, Blaisdell, Waltham, Massachusetts.

HOROWITZ, E. L. (1965), 'Development of attitudes towards Negroes', in H. Proshansky and B. Seidenberg (eds.), *Basic Studies in Social Psychology*, Holt, Rinehart & Winston, pp. 111–21.

HORTON, R. E. (1963), 'American freedom and the values of youth', in H. H. Remmers (ed.), *Anti-Democratic Attitudes in American Schools*, North-Western University Press, pp. 18–60.

HUDSON, L. (1966), *Contrary Imaginations*, Methuen; Penguin, 1967.

HUDSON, L. (1967), 'The stereotypical scientist', *Nature*, vol. 213, no. 5073, pp. 228–9.

HUDSON, L. (1968), *Frames of Mind*, Methuen; Penguin, 1970.

HUME, R. (1968), 'The effects of school and curriculum on boys' attitudes towards careers in engineering', *Brit. J. educ. Psychol.*, vol. 38, pp. 322–3.

HUNT, J. McV. (1960), 'Experience and the development of motivation: some reinterpretations', *Child Dev.*, vol. 31, pp. 489–504.

HUNT, J. McV. (1961), *Intelligence and Experience*, Ronald Press.

HUNT, J. McV. (1969), 'Has compensatory education failed? Has it been attempted?' *Harv. educ. Rev.*, vol. 39, pp. 278–300.

HYMAN, H. (1959), *Political Socialization*, Free Press.

INNER LONDON EDUCATION AUTHORITY (1967a), *The Education of Immigrant Pupils in Primary Schools*.

INNER LONDON EDUCATION AUTHORITY (1967b), *London Comprehensive Schools, 1966*.

JACKSON, B. (1964), *Streaming: An Educational System in Miniature*, Routledge & Kegan Paul.

JACKSON, B., and MARSDEN, D. (1962), *Education and the Working Class*, Routledge & Kegan Paul; Penguin, 1966.

JAHODA, G. (1952), 'Job attitudes and job choice among secondary modern school leavers', *Occup. Psychol.*, vol. 26, pp. 125–40, 206–24.

JAHODA, G. (1963), 'The development of children's ideas about country and nationality', *Brit. J. educ. Psychol.*, vol. 33, pp. 47–60, 143–53.

JAHODA, G., and CHALMERS, A. D. (1963), 'The Youth Employment Service: consumer perspective'. *Occup. Psychol.*, vol. 37, pp. 40–43.

JAMES, H. E. O., and TENEN, C. (1953), *The Teacher was Black*, Heinemann.

JAROS, D., HIRSCH, H., and FLERON, F. J. (1968), 'The malevolent leader: political socialization in an American sub-culture', *Amer. polit. Sci. Rev.*, vol. 62, pp. 564–615.

JENSEN, A. R. (1969), 'How much can we boost I.Q. and scholastic achievement?', *Harv. educ. Rev.*, vol. 39, pp. 1–123.

JOHNSON, N. (1966), 'Children's comics', *New Soc.*, vol. 8, no. 197, pp. 7–12.

JONES, W. R. (1966), *Bilingualism in Welsh Education*, University of Wales Press.

KAGAN, J., and MOSS, H. A. (1959), 'Stability and validity of achievement fantasy'. *J. abnorm. soc. Psychol.*, vol. 58, pp. 357–64.

KAWWA, T. (1968), 'A survey of ethnic attitudes of some British secondary school pupils', *Brit. J. soc. clin. Psychol.*, vol. 7, pp. 161–8.

KELLEY, H. H. (1950), 'The warm–cold variable in first impressions of persons', *J. Personal.*, vol. 18, pp. 431–9.

KELLMER PRINGLE, M. L. (1966), *Social Learning and its Measurement*, Longman.

KELLMER PRINGLE, M. L., and EDWARDS, J. (1964), 'Some moral concepts and judgements of junior school children', *Brit. J. soc. clin. Psychol.*, vol. 3, pp. 196–215.

KELLMER PRINGLE, M. L., BUTLER, N. R., and DAVIS, R. (1966), *11,000 Seven-Year-Olds*, Longman.

KEMP, L. C. D. (1955), 'Environmental and other characteristics determining attainments in primary schools', *Brit. J. educ. Psychol.*, vol. 25, pp. 67–77.

KENNEDY, W. A., and WILLCUTT, H. C. (1964), 'Praise and blame as incentives', *Psychol. Bull.*, vol. 62, pp. 323–32.

KENT JENNINGS, M., and NIEMI, R. G. (1968a), 'Patterns of political learning', *Harv. educ. Rev.*, vol. 38, pp. 443–67.

KENT JENNINGS, M., and NIEMI, R. G. (1968b), 'The transmission of political values from parent to child', *Amer. polit. Sci. Rev.*, vol. 62, pp. 169–84.

KINNANE, J. F., and PABLE, M. W. (1962), 'Family background and work value orientation', *J. counsel. Psychol.*, vol. 9, pp. 320–25.

KLEIN, J. (1965), *Samples from English Culture*, vols. 1 and 2, Routledge & Kegan Paul.

KOHLBERG, L. (1963), 'Moral development and identification', in H. Stevenson (ed.), *Child Psychology*, University of Chicago Press.

KOHLBERG, L. (1966), 'Development of moral character and ideology', in L. Hoffman and M. Hoffman (eds.), *Review of Child Development Research*, vol. 1, Russell Sage Foundation, New York, pp. 383–431.

KRATHWOHL, D. R., BLOOM, B. S., and MASIA, B. B. (1964), *Taxonomy of Educational Objectives. II: Affective Domain*, Longman.

LAMBERT, W. E., and KLINEBERG, O. (1967), *Children's Views of Foreign Peoples*, Appleton-Century-Crofts.

LANE, R. E. (1968), 'Political education in the midst of life's struggles', *Harv. educ. Rev.*, vol. 38, pp. 468–94.

LANGTON, K. P. (1967), 'Peer group and school and the political socialization process', *Amer. polit. Sci. Rev.*, vol. 61, pp. 751–8.

LANGTON, K. P., and KENT JENNINGS, M. (1968), 'Political socialization and the high school civics curriculum in the United States', *Amer. polit. Sci. Rev.*, vol. 62, pp. 852–67.

LAVIN, D. E. (1965), *The Prediction of Academic Performance*, Wiley.

LAWTON, D. (1968), *Social Class, Language and Education*, Routledge & Kegan Paul.

LOBAN, W. D. (1963), *The Language of Elementary School Children*, National Council of Teachers of English, Research Report no. 1, Champaign, Illinois.

LOVELL, K., and WHITE, G. E. (1958), 'Some influences affecting choice of subjects in school and training college', *Brit. J. educ. Psychol.*, vol. 28, pp. 15–24.

MCCLELLAND, D. C., ATKINSON, J. W., CLARK, R. A., and LOWELL, E. L. (1953), *The Achievement Motive*, Appleton-Century-Crofts.

MCCLINTOCK, G. G., and TURNER, H. A. (1962), 'The impact of college upon political knowledge, participation and values', *Hum. Rel.*, vol. 15, pp. 163–76.

MACFARLANE, J., ALLEN, L., and HONZIK, N. (1954), *A Developmental Study of Behavior Problems of Normal Children between 21 Months and Four Years*, University of California Press.

MCINTOSH, D. M., and EWAN, E. A. (1970), 'Timetabling. I: How to make the most of subject, talent and inclination', *Times educ. Supp. (Scot.)*, no. 225, 2 January; II: Subject compatibility in the larger group', ibid., no. 226, 9 January.

MCINTYRE, D., and MORRISON, A. (1967), 'A comparative study of the attitudes of African and Scottish students towards African affairs', unpublished study (available from the authors).

MACNAMARA, J. (1966), *Bilingualism and Primary Education*, Edinburgh University Press.

MACCOBY, E. E., and WHITING, J. W. (1960), 'Some child-rearing correlates of young children's responses to deviation stories', unpublished study, Stanford University.

MADSEN, C., BECKER, W. C., and THOMAS, D. R. (1968), 'Rules, praise and ignoring: elements of elementary classroom control', *J. appl. behav. Anal.*, vol. 1, pp. 139–50.

MAINER, R. E. (1963), 'Attitude change in inter-group education programs', in H. H. Remmers (ed.), *Anti-Democratic Attitudes in American Schools*, North-Western University Press, pp. 122–54.

MEREI, F. (1949), 'Group leadership and institutionalization', *Hum. Rel.*, vol. 2, pp. 23–9.

MEYER, G. R., and PENFOLD, D. M. E. (1961), 'Factors associated with interest in science', *Brit. J. educ. Psychol.*, vol. 31, pp. 33–7.

MILLER, T. W. G. (1961), *Values in the Comprehensive School*, Oliver & Boyd.

MISCHEL, W. (1963), 'Delay of gratification and deviant behavior', paper read at meeting of the Society for Research in Child Development, Berkeley, California.

MITCHELL, J. V. (1961), 'An analysis of the factorial dimensions of the achievement motivation construct', *J. educ. Psychol.*, vol. 52, pp. 179–87.

MORRISON, A. (1967), 'Attitudes of children towards international affairs', *Educ. Res.*, pp. 197–202.

MORRISON, A., and HALLWORTH, H. J. (1966), 'The perception of peer personality by adolescent girls', *Brit. J. educ. Psychol.*, vol. 36, pp. 241–7.

MORTON-WILLIAMS, R., and FINCH, S. (1968), *Schools Council, Enquiry 1: Young School Leavers*, HMSO.

NACHMANN, B. (1960), 'Childhood experience and vocational choice in law, dentistry and social work', *J. counsel. Psychol.*, vol. 7, pp. 243–50.

NEWCOMB, T. M. (1965), 'Attitude development as a function of reference groups: the Bennington study', in H. Proshansky and B. Seidenberg (eds.), *Basic Studies in Social Psychology*, Holt, Rinehart & Winston, pp. 215–25.

NEWMAN, F. M. (1968), 'Political socialization in the schools', *Harv. educ. Rev.*, vol. 38, pp. 536–45.

Newsom Report (1963), *Half Our Future*, Report of the Central Advisory Council for Education (England), HMSO.

NEWSON, J., and NEWSON, E. (1968), 'Some social differences in the process of childrearing' in J. Gould (ed.), *Penguin Social Sciences Survey 1968*, Penguin, pp. 74–97.

NISBET, J. D. (1961), 'Family environment and intelligence', in A. H. Halsey, J. Floud and C. A. Anderson (eds.), *Education, Economy and Society*, Free Press, pp. 273–287.

O'HARA, R. P., and TIEDEMANN, D. V. (1959), 'Vocational self-concept in adolescence', *J. counsel. Psychol.*, vol. 6, pp. 292–301.

OPPENHEIMER, E. A. (1966), 'The relationship between certain self-constructs and occupational preferences', *J. counsel. Psychol.*, vol. 13, pp. 191–7.

OSIPOW, S. H. (1968), *Theories of Career Development*, Appleton-Century-Crofts.

OSIPOW, S. H., ASHBY, J. D., and WALL, H. W. (1966), 'Personality types and vocational choice: a test of Holland's theory', *Personn. Guid. J.*, vol. 45, pp. 37–42.

OXFORD UNIVERSITY DEPARTMENT OF EDUCATION (1963), *Technology and the Sixth Form Boy*.

PAPE, G. V. (1961), 'Mixing in the comprehensive school', *For. Educ.*, vol. 3, pp. 71–4.

PATON, X., and BELOFF, H. (1970), 'Bronfenbrenner's moral dilemmas in Britain: children, their peers and parents', *Int. J. Psychol.*, vol. 5, pp. 27–32.

PEAKER, G. F. (1967), 'The regression analyses of the national survey', in *Children and their Primary Schools*, (*Plowden Report*), Report of the Central Advisory Council for Education (England), HMSO, app. 4.

PEARCE, R. A. (1958), 'Streaming and a sociometric study', *Educ. Rev.*, vol. 10, pp. 248–51.

PIAGET, J. (1932), *The Moral Judgement of the Child*, Routledge & Kegan Paul.

PIAGET, J., and WEILL, A. M. (1951), 'The development in children of the idea of the homeland and of relations with other countries', *Inter. soc. Sci. Bull.*, vol. 3.

PONT, H. B., and BUTCHER, H. J. (1968), 'Choice of course and subject specialization in seventeen Scottish secondary schools', *Scot. educ. Stud.*, vol. 1, pp. 9–15.

PRITCHARD, R. A. (1935), 'The relative popularity of secondary school subjects at various ages', *Brit. J. educ. Psychol.*, vol. 5, pp. 157–79, 229–41.

RADKE, M., TRAGER, H. G., and DAVIS, H. (1949), 'Social perceptions and attitudes of children', *Genet. psychol. Monogr.*, vol. 40, pp. 327–447.

RIST, R. C. (1970), 'Student social class and teacher expectations: the self-fulfilling prophecy in ghetto education', *Harv. educ. Rev.*, vol. 40, pp. 411–51.

Robbins Report (1963), *Higher Education*, Report of the Committee Appointed by the Prime Minister under the Chairmanship of Lord Robbins, 1961–3, HMSO, Cmnd 2154.

ROBINSON, W. P., and RACKSTRAW, S. J. (1967), 'Variations in mothers' answers to children's questions as a function of social class, verbal intelligence test scores, and sex', *Sociology*, vol. 1, pp. 259–76.

ROE, A. (1956), *The Psychology of Occupations*, Wiley.

ROE, A. (1957), 'Early determinants of vocational choice', *J. counsel. Psychol.*, vol. 4, pp. 212–17.

ROE, A., and SIEGELMAN, M. (1964), *The Origin of Interests*, American Personnel and Guidance Association, Inquiry Study, Washington DC.

ROGOFF, N. (1961), 'Local social structure and educational selection', in A. H. Halsey, J. Floud and C. A. Anderson (eds.), *Education, Economy and Society*, Free Press.

ROSEN, B. C. (1956), 'The achievement syndrome: a psycho-cultural dimension of social stratification', *Amer. sociol. Rev.*, vol. 21, pp. 203–11.

ROSEN, B. C., and D'ANDRADE, R. (1959), 'The psycho-social origins of achievement motivation', *Sociometry*, vol. 22, pp. 185–218.

ROSEN, C. (1948), 'The effect of the motion picture "Gentleman's Agreement" on attitudes towards Jews', *J. Psychol.*, vol. 26, pp. 525–36.

ROSEN, M., (1961), 'Valence, expectancy and dissonance reduction in the prediction of goal striving', paper presented at meeting of the Eastern Psychological Association, Pennsylvania, April. Reprinted in V. H. Vroom (ed.), *Work and Motivation*, Wiley, 1964, pp. 75–81.

ROSENBERG, M. (1957), *Occupations and Values*, Free Press.

ROSNOW, R. L., and ROBINSON, E. J. (1967), *Experiments in Persuasion*, Academic Press.

ROTHENBERG, B. B. (1968), *Children's Social Sensitivity and the Relationship to Interpersonal Competence, Intrapersonal Comfort and Intellectual Level*, Research Bulletin, Educational Testing Service, Princeton, New Jersey.

RUTHERFORD, J. (1966), 'An investigation into some aspects of political awareness in a sample of secondary school boys', M. Ed. thesis, University of Birmingham.

SCHOFIELD, M. (1968), *The Sexual Behaviour of Young People*, Penguin.

SEARS, D. O. (1968), '"The development of political attitudes in children", by R. D. Hess and J. Thorney', *Harv. educ. Rev.*, vol. 38, pp. 571–7.

SHAKESPEARE, J. J. (1936), 'An enquiry into the relative popularity of school subjects in elementary schools', *Brit. J. educ. Psychol.*, vol. 6, pp. 147–64.

SHIELS, A. (1970), 'Children's concept of the law', unpublished dissertation, Edinburgh University.

SIEGEL, A., and SIEGEL, S. (1957), 'Reference groups, membership groups and attitude change', *J. abnorm. soc. Psychol.*, vol. 95, pp. 360–64.

SIGEL, R. S. (1968), 'Image of a President: some insights into political views of school children', *Amer. polit. Sci. Rev.*, vol. 62, pp. 216–25.

SINGER, D. (1961), 'Verbal conditioning and generalizations of pro-democratic responses', *J. abnorm. soc. Psychol.*, vol. 63, pp. 43–6.

SINGER, D. (1964), 'The impact of interracial exposure on the social attitudes of fifth-grade children', unpublished study, reported in H. M. Proshansky 'The development of intergroup attitudes', in L. W. Hoffman and M. L. Hoffman (eds.), *Review of Child*

Development Research, Russell Sage Foundation, New York, 1966, pp. 311–71.

SOARES, A., and SOARES, L. (1969), 'Self-perceptions of culturally disadvantaged children', *Amer. educ. Res. J.*, vol. 6, pp. 31–45.

STEPHENSON, R. R. (1961), 'Occupational choice as a crystallized self-concept', *J. counsel. Psychol.*, vol. 8, pp. 211–16.

STEVENSON, H. W., KEEN, R., and KNIGHTS, R. M. (1963), 'Parents and strangers as reinforcing agents for children's performance', *J. abnorm. soc. Psychol.*, vol. 67, pp. 183–6.

STOKES, D. E. (1964), 'Ideological competition of British parties', paper delivered at 1964 Annual Meeting of the American Political Science Association, Chicago, Illinois.

STRODTBECK, F. L. (1958), 'Family interaction, values and achievement', in D. C. McClelland, A. L. Baldwin, U. Bronfenbrenner and F. L. Strodtbeck (eds.), *Talent and Society*, Van Nostrand, pp. 135–94.

STRONG, E. K. (1943), *Vocational Interests of Men and Women*, Stanford University Press.

SUGARMAN, B. (1967), 'Involvement in youth culture, academic achievement and conformity in school', *Brit. J. Soc.*, vol. 18, pp. 151–64.

SUPER, D. E. (1953), 'A theory of vocational development', *Amer. Psychol.*, vol. 8, pp. 185–90.

SUPER, D. E., and OVERSTREET, P. L. (1960), *The Vocational Maturity of Ninth Grade Boys*, Teachers College, Columbia University.

SUPER, D. E., STAVISHEVSKY, R., MATLIN, N., and JORDAAN, J. P. (1963), *Career Development: Self-Concept Theory*, College Entrance Examination Board, Research Monograph, New York.

SVENSSON, N. E. (1962), *Ability Grouping and Scholastic Achievement*, Urbana, Stockholm.

SWIFT, D. F. (1964), 'Who passes the 11 + ?', *New Soc.*, vol. 3, no. 75, pp. 6–9.

SWIFT, D. F. (1967), 'Family environment and 11 + success: some basic predictions', *Brit. J. educ. Psychol.*, vol. 37, pp. 10–21.

TAJFEL, H. (1966), 'Children and nationalism', *New Soc.*, vol. 7, no. 196, pp. 9–11.

TENNYSON, W. W. (1968), 'Career development', *Rev. educ. Res.*, vol. 38, pp. 346–66.

THORNDIKE, R. L., and HAGEN, E. (1959), *Ten Thousand Careers*, Wiley.

TYLER, L. (1951), 'The relationship of interests to attitudes and reputations among first-grade children', *Educ. psychol. Meas.*, vol. 11, pp. 255–64.

TYLER, L. (1964), 'The antecedents of two varieties of vocational interests', *Genet. psychol. Monogr.*, vol. 70, pp. 177–227.

VERNON, P. E. (1969), *Intelligence and Cultural Environment*, Methuen.

WALLACE, W. L. (1966), *Student Culture*, Aldine.

WALSH, R. P. (1959), 'The effect of needs on responses to job duties', *J. counsel. Psychol.*, vol. 6, pp. 194–8.

WARBURTON, F. W. (1964), 'Attainment and the school environment', in S. Wiseman (ed.), *Education and Environment*, Manchester University Press, pp. 101–25.

WARR, P., SCHRODER, H. M., and BLACKMAN, S. (1969), 'The structure of political judgement', *Brit. J. soc. clin. Psychol.*, vol. 8, pp. 32–43.

WARREN, J. R. (1961), 'Self concept, occupational role expectations and change in college major', *J. counsel. Psychol.*, vol. 8, pp. 164–9.

WEBSTER, H., FREEDMAN, N., and HEIST, P. (1962), 'Personality changes in college students', in N. Sanford (ed.), *The American College*, Wiley, pp. 805–46.

WERTS, C. E. (1968), 'Parental influence on career choice', *J. counsel. Psychol.*, vol. 15, pp. 48–52.

WILSON, A. B. (1959), 'Residential segregation of social classes and aspirations of high school boys', *Amer. sociol. Rev.*, vol. 24, pp. 836–45.

WILSON, J., WILLIAMS, N., and SUGARMAN, B. (1967), *Introduction to Moral Education*, Penguin.

WISEMAN, S. (1964), *Education and Environment*, Manchester University Press.

WISEMAN, S. (1967), 'The Manchester Survey', in *Children and their Primary Schools*, (*Plowden Report*), Report of the Central Advisory Council for Education (England), HMSO, app. 9.

WISEMAN, S. (1968), 'Educational deprivation and disadvantage', in H. J. Butcher (ed.), *Educational Research in Britain*, University of London Press, pp. 261–81.

YOUNG, M., and McGEENEY, P. (1968), *Learning Begins at Home*, Routledge & Kegan Paul.

ZAJONC, R. B. (1966), *Social Psychology: An Experimental Approach*, Wadsworth.

ZILLER, R. C. (1957), 'Vocational choice and utility for risk', *J. counsel. Psychol.*, vol. 4, pp. 61–4.

Index